Advance praise for *A Man Called Mark*

"Bishop Mark Dyer was a gentle, affirming, caring human being with an inbuilt moral compass pointing in the direction of Ubuntu. His appreciation of our interdependence, that we are made for each other—God-carriers all, none superior, none inferior, and none more or less entitled—inevitably placed him on the righteous side of church discussions on contentious issues; the side of the disregarded, marginalized, ostracized, and oppressed."

—Archbishop Emeritus Desmond Tutu

"If you ever had the pleasure of speaking with Mark Dyer, Tom Linthicum's book will allow you to relive it. Here is the same clarity and generosity. Here complex issues are made easier to understand. And here is the same low-keyed sparkle that made Bishop Dyer simultaneously charismatic and unassuming. In both tone and content, *A Man Called Mark* is an experience of the man."

—Jim Naughton, Canticle Communications

"One of the best ways to read history is to read biography. And this book is the perfect example. Through the remarkable life of Bishop Mark Dyer, the reader learns about the history of the Episcopal Church, the Anglican Communion, twentieth-century Ecumenism, and the challenges of theological education. Beautifully written, this book invites one into a remarkable world of faith, hope, and love."

—The Very Rev. Ian Markham, President and Dean of Virginia Theological Seminary

"Mark Dyer was very much a gift to the church at home and abroad. His theological reflection was deeply rooted in his faith and bore witness to the words of Evagrius: 'A theologian is one who prays.' As a bishop, Mark was a pastor after the manner of the abbot in the Rule of St. Benedict—able to listen to different voices with care, compassion, and discernment. *A Man Called Mark* allows those of us who knew him to know him, perhaps, more fully, and for others to meet this wise and seasoned man of the Spirit for the first time."

—The Most Rev. Frank T. Griswold, XXV
Presiding Bishop of the Episcopal Church

"For someone who only knew Mark at the end of his life, this book opened my eyes to how influential he was in the broader church. Tom Linthicum masterfully captures the captivating and Spirit-filled relationships and stories of Bishop Mark Dyer's holy life."

—The Rev. Christopher Miller, rector of Immanuel
Episcopal Church in Mechanicsville, Maryland

"A beautiful and inspiring story of beloved Bishop Mark Dyer, a true witness in the 'cloud of witnesses.' This book brilliantly illuminates how his life lived in deep faith continues to radiate through those who knew him, who were taught and mentored by him, and especially those who shared a part of his journey and had the privilege to pray with him. A must read; the theological values and principles he developed and taught are vital to the continued transformation of the church today."

—The Very Rev. Robyn Szoke-Coolidge, Dean, Stevenson
School for Ministry, Diocese of Central Pennsylvania

A Man
Called Mark

THE BIOGRAPHY OF
BISHOP MARK DYER

Tom Linthicum

Foreword by *Rowan Williams*

CHURCH
PUBLISHING
INCORPORATED

Church Publishing
19 East 34th Street
New York, NY 10016
www.churchpublishing.org

Cover photo courtesy of The Episcopal Diocese of Bethlehem
Cover design by Jennifer Kopec, 2Pug Design
Typeset by PerfecType, Nashville, Tennessee

Library of Congress Cataloging-in-Publication Data

A record of this book is available from the Library of Congress.

ISBN-13: 978-1-64065-097-8 (pbk.)
ISBN-13: 978-1-64065-098-5 (ebook)

Printed in the United States of America

I am so very grateful that Mark's life touched mine; that friendship bloomed into late love. His spirit, his love for God was evident every day of our life together. Whenever I would feel defeated about some event or interaction that happened, Mark would tell me that his job was to convince me that God loved me just the way I am, even if it took the rest of our lives. I felt loved and cared for by Mark, and that love will always be in my heart.

I pray that this book will be an inspiration to those who knew him and loved him, and that his love for God will be shared in a way that they, too, will know that God loves them just the way they are.

Thanks be to God for this man called Mark.

Amy Dyer
June 2017
Alexandria, Virginia

CONTENTS

FOREWORD

Reading this vivid and affectionate memoir brought back with great clarity my memories of Bishop Mark, and I know that it will do just the same for many more readers. But what struck me most was not the very full account of all the diverse projects which Mark steered forward on behalf of the Anglican Communion, but his determination to minister—as priest and bishop—as if the theology he believed in were actually true.

That's not to say that no one else did or does that; but most of us are uneasily conscious that the way we perform our ministerial tasks is not always something that allows the theology we believe to shine through, and that we take for granted styles and habits of doing this that are—as you might say—not completely "converted." We do it like this because this is how it's done, and it's a bit too much trouble to start over and rethink what our ministry would have to look like in order to point to the theology that most matters to us.

Mark approached things differently. His monastic formation had penetrated to the deepest DNA of his ministry as priest and bishop, so that he was never able to walk away from the charismatic and communal example of authority that the Rule of Saint Benedict assumes. It could be a practical challenge for colleagues, as the narrative here makes plain! But it was also a challenge of a much deeper and more important kind, provoking the church to ask why and how theology and the life of common prayer really mattered; because if it did matter as much as someone like Mark presupposed, it ought to be visible in the way we do things to a far larger extent than it usually is.

In a suspicious and sometimes ungracious atmosphere, it is all too easy to think that if you believe in the seriousness of theology and the need for the church to reflect the character of revealed truth in its actual daily dealings and structures, then you are somehow an enemy of liberty or autonomy. The most poignant pages in this book are those that describe the hostility Mark experienced from people in his own much-loved church to some of his efforts to commend a more integrally theological approach to the handling of the bitter conflicts of the last few decades.

You may be skeptical about some of these efforts; but the angry dismissal of them as implicitly totalitarian represented a failure to see the positive and necessary point being made—which is that *how* the church manages conflict and authority is part of its proclamation of Christ's gospel, and that the admission of interdependent responsibility is not a humiliating abdication of Christian liberty. For Mark, with his consistent mistrust of clerical power games and fantasies, the charge of being caught up in simply another such power game was a bitter one indeed, and these pages leave us in no doubt of the cost to him.

Whatever you make of the various recent attempts to create better structures of mutual accountability in the Anglican family, there is an underlying issue that won't go away, to do with the church's integrity. That was what Mark was concerned with, and it was the reluctance to acknowledge the spiritual gravity of the issue that he found hurtful and frustrating. Yet, in God's providence, he was able to communicate what he most deeply cared about in so many other ways, above all as a teacher, a true *starets* to so many at Virginia Theological Seminary and beyond (and this book rightly celebrates the vision and generosity of the seminary as well as celebrating Mark himself). Like a good spiritual father, he "wrote in souls." It is not the essays and the reports that are most important but the imprint of a vision lived out in a person, the lives, the ministries made possible through his witness.

This welcome book allows that imprint to be made afresh on the minds and hearts of many who never met Mark. He helped so many of us see something of what Anglican identity could be at its most generous and positive, and indeed what ecumenical might be when it was not a matter of negotiated platitudes and cautious practical collaboration. He was and he remains a sign of hope for the Anglican family, which owes him far more than it knows.

+Rowan Williams
Cambridge

PROLOGUE

January 30, 2007, was a typical winter day in London—chilly and overcast with light rain. But there was nothing typical about the occasion being observed there that day by leaders of the world's second and third largest Christian traditions. Bartholomew I, the Ecumenical Patriarch of the Eastern Orthodox Church with its 200 million members, and Rowan Williams, Archbishop of Canterbury and head of the Anglican Communion with its 70 million members, were assembled with a host of other dignitaries.

After seventeen years of painstaking theological dialogue, Orthodox and Anglican representatives had produced a ground-breaking document, *The Church of the Triune God*, which established new areas of agreement and opened the door for continued talks on such intractable issues as the ordination of women. Steeped in history and tradition, the day began with a ceremony at Lambeth Palace, home of the Archbishop of Canterbury since the thirteenth century, and ended with Evensong at Westminster Abbey, site of every British coronation since 1066.

At the center of this ecclesiastical pomp and circumstance was Mark Dyer, a soft-spoken, unassuming American Episcopal bishop who was co-author and architect of the historic theological statement along with Metropolitan John Zizioulas of Pergamon, his Eastern Orthodox counterpart. Now retired from being a clergyman and seminary professor, Dyer was there with his wife, Amy, to rejoice with his colleagues in the fruits of their labor. As a token of gratitude for his efforts, he would receive one of the highest awards the Anglican Communion could bestow.

In many ways, Dyer was an unlikely protagonist in this drama playing out on a world stage. A former Benedictine monk who was raised in the bluest of blue-collar Catholic neighborhoods and became bishop of a small Episcopal diocese in Pennsylvania coal country, he was nonetheless known and respected by many of the world's religious leaders.

For two decades, Dyer moved at the highest levels of Anglican theology and diplomacy, shaping relations with other traditions and influencing policy on divisive issues, most notably the role of women as clergy and the church's position on same-sex relationships. At the same time, he provided transformational leadership and spiritual guidance for his diocese while also inspiring and mentoring countless bishops, priests, and seminary students who treasured their relationships with him.

His was a life of profound faith and spiritual depth freely shared. For all of its joys and triumphs, it was also punctuated with disappointments and tragedies. Yet through it all, Dyer embraced all life had to offer, bearing witness to the healing power of God's love and serving as a model for others.

It was a remarkable journey that began with a most humble beginning.

CHAPTER 1

"You Are Irish Catholic"

As I look at my faith and the oppression our family had to
go through during the Herbert Hoover days and what the
church did, that was very moving to me.[1] —Mark Dyer

Times were tough—very tough indeed—when James Michael
Dyer Jr. entered the world on June 7, 1930, in Manchester, New
Hampshire.

It was the first year of the Great Depression. The stock mar-
ket had crashed the previous October, and the country was reeling
from the hammer blows of an imploding economy. Unemployment
lines stretched endlessly, banks were failing, savings were deci-
mated. Manchester, a mill town founded in 1846 on the banks of the
Merrimack River fifty miles north of Boston, was hit especially hard.
Its decline had begun in the 1920s as its mills, which once included
the largest cotton textile mill complex in the world, began to falter.

The world as Manchester had known it ended on Christmas Eve,
1935, when the last mill closed and filed for bankruptcy. At one time
its owner had employed seventeen thousand people and was the chief

1

source of income for half of Manchester's families.² Stunned by their city's economic collapse, Manchester's nearly seventy-seven thousand residents did whatever they could to get by.

In the household of the Dyer family, an Irish clan rooted in the Roman Catholic Church, traditional values of family, faith, and work reigned supreme. That included the illegal making and selling of whiskey since Prohibition was the law of the land. Everyone pitched in, even the new baby. It was a story—confirmed by his younger sister, Pat Cashin—that Dyer always took great relish in telling. "My grandfather made it in the cellar," he said, referring to the forbidden brew. "Then he would make the deliveries in the baby carriage, which he had modified with a place for the bottles underneath, and I was the baby in that carriage."³ And so the carriage bounced along the streets of Manchester, with the youngest Dyer nestled atop the bottles, providing a very legitimate cover for a very illegitimate operation. The first stop was always the residence of the monsignor, who would get a complimentary bottle. There was also a free bottle for the cop on the beat—a good Irishman, of course.

As Dyer grew up during these times of great hardship, he saw firsthand how the Catholic Church ministered to its parishioners not just on Sundays but every day, helping people survive and giving them hope. "The monsignor always knew who was working and who wasn't, which families were struggling the most, and he would send over money or food when it was most needed," Dyer recalled many years later. "It was a social welfare system, it was run by the church, and it worked."⁴

It was a lesson Dyer never forgot. It provided the foundation for his lifelong commitment to social justice and his belief in the church's calling to serve the poor. For Jimmy Dyer, as he was called by his family (Mark was the name he would later take as a young monk), life in Manchester, even in times of deprivation, was a rich tapestry of family, church, and the Irish community.

His father, James M. Dyer, worked as a baker by day and made bread at St. Patrick's Orphanage for Girls at night. "On Friday night he would make what the children would like on Saturday morning, and he would bake cookies," said Pat. "He would make all kinds of cakes for people, and he never asked for any money. He was a good man."[5]

Anna Mahoney Dyer raised Jimmy and Pat, cared for her husband's ailing parents, and took in sewing work to help meet expenses. The four Dyers, along with James Dyer's parents, Anna's mother, and other family members, shared a rambling, three-story house at 352 Cedar Street, in the Irish and Greek quarter of the inner city's east side. "There was no money but there were good times," said Pat. "Grandfather Dyer went to church every morning at 7, and Grandmother was in her rocking chair, saying her rosary. At 6:30, [Jimmy and I] would fire up the oil furnace. Then we would have oatmeal, toast, and orange juice, and leave for school.

"For fun after dinner, sometimes we would sit on the front steps. Other times, we would listen to jazz and do the jitterbug. On weekends, if we were lucky, we would go to the movies and watch cowboy movies on Saturday afternoons but never on Sunday. Sunday was Mass at 9 or 10:30 and then breakfast and a big dinner—roast beef, fried chicken, mashed potatoes, and vegetables—at 1."[6]

Every year when the circus came to town, nobody in Manchester was more excited than Jimmy Dyer. He would jump out of bed between 3 and 4 in the morning to watch the elephants lumber from their railroad cars to the circus venue; he was convinced that this was the greatest form of free entertainment known to man.

No matter how tight things were, Agnes Mahoney (Anna's mother) managed to scrape together enough money every year to rent a cottage for a two-week family vacation at Hampton Beach, located on southeast New Hampshire's eighteen-mile sliver of craggy Atlantic coastline. Those memorable trips kindled Dyer's lifelong love affair with the sea.

The family's Irish roots ran deep. Grandparents on both sides were born in Ireland. Years later while he was studying in Belgium, Dyer would visit the family farm in the village of Farranfore, near Killarney in County Kerry, before it became an airport. Anna Dyer treasured her Irish heritage so much that when she died in 1995, the local funeral home flew the Irish flag in her honor.

The Irish-American Club, a tired, one-room affair with a bar, some worn chairs, and a sagging floor, was not far from the home on Cedar Street. Dyer's father would go there regularly on Fridays and Saturdays, and as Jimmy grew older, he would meet his friends there as well.

Although Jimmy developed a taste for beer when he came of age, Anna Dyer was a confirmed teetotaler and a member of the Pioneer Total Abstinence Association of the Sacred Heart, founded in Dublin in 1898. Dyer told a friend years later that on one occasion, fearful that an Irish wake in her home was getting out of hand, his mother emptied all of the whiskey bottles into the sink, bringing the gathering to an abrupt halt.

The Catholic Church was also a defining influence in Dyer's life. "Grandmother would say to us, 'You are Irish Catholic,'" Pat recalled, as if the two were woven seamlessly together. During Dyer's early years, they were.[7] His family attended St. Anne's Church, a bastion of Irish Catholicism, where he was baptized on June 21, 1930. The Dyers attended church every Sunday, and young Jimmy became an altar boy and attended Catholic schools.

Tragedy struck the Dyer family when Jimmy was fifteen. Born with only one kidney, his father was stricken at home one evening in January 1946 with a terrible stomachache. He was taken to the hospital, where doctors discovered a virulent infection in his remaining kidney that they were powerless to stop. He died that night at the age of thirty-nine.

More than half a century later, Mark told his wife, Amy, whom he married in 2004, about his memories from that traumatic time: "I learned so much about my father that I didn't know as I wandered from room to room at the wake. The women were in the kitchen, saying how kind and caring my father had been, telling about his care for the nuns and doing their baking after he finished his work. The men were in the parlor telling funny stories about him, always with a good Irish punch line. One story stayed with me, about how my grandmother would always call my father downstairs to break up fights between my uncles and how he was the one who looked after my Uncle Matthew when he'd had too much to drink. I learned a lot about my father that night."[8]

His father's death was a crushing blow to Jimmy Dyer. Always a good student, his grades plummeted and his mother had to intercede with his teachers. In time, Dyer regained his emotional equilibrium and his grades returned to normal. But the life he had known was over. Young Jimmy Dyer was now the man of the house.

Despite the Catholic Church's central role in Dyer's life, there was never any talk in those years of his becoming a priest. Many years later, he said that if he had given much thought to a future vocation at that point in his life, he probably would have said he wanted to be a firefighter or a policeman because that's what most Irishmen did in Manchester.

"[Our mother] didn't want him to be a priest and she didn't want me to be a nun," said Pat. "She thought he would have to go far away."[9]

It turned out that he did go far away, but it wasn't the church that took him there. It was the church that brought him back.

CHAPTER 2

War and Monasteries

When I was on shore in Greece, I was taking my turn as an MP, watching out for the guys who had a bit too much to drink. This one kid started a fight and the local police picked him up. Some of the guys he was with came to get me and tell me that he was at the police station, so I went up there, not really knowing what to do. When I got there, they were, of course, speaking Greek. I knew enough Greek from the guys I grew up with in Manchester that I could tell this kid was in big trouble. So I just started to chat with them in what street Greek I knew. The cops looked at me and said, "You Greek? Get this guy out of here!" We took off quickly before they changed their minds.[1] —Mark Dyer

The nation was still catching its breath from World War II when a new conflict broke out on the other side of the world from Manchester. It was the Korean War, and it would radically change Jimmy Dyer's life.

Too young to serve in World War II—he was fifteen when it ended—Dyer graduated from St. Joseph's Cathedral High School in 1948 and worked various jobs in Manchester, delivering newspapers and driving a truck for the city. Still living at home, he contributed his income to help support the household and enjoyed the postwar rhythms of life with family and friends.

But things began to change on June 25, 1950, when North Korean soldiers poured across the 38th parallel into South Korea. The United States was soon drawn into the war. More soldiers, sailors, and airmen were needed, and volunteers and draftees would fill the ranks.

Dyer wanted to choose his branch of service, so on January 17, 1951, he went to Boston and enlisted in the navy.[2] This offered him a four-year, all-expenses-paid tour of exotic ports of call and more money than he was making in Manchester—most of which he would send home to his mother.

With all hell breaking loose on the rugged Korean Peninsula, Dyer found himself at the Naval Training Center in Newport, Rhode Island,[3] with its yacht-filled harbor and Gilded Age mansions. He and his naval aviation unit prepared for combat in a remote locale that he, like most Americans, knew virtually nothing about.

On May 10, 1952, Dyer's Fighter Squadron 71 (VF-71) flew to San Francisco, where it was assigned to the aircraft carrier USS *Bon Homme Richard*, namesake of the famous warship commanded by John Paul Jones in the Revolutionary War. Ten days later, the "Bonnie Dick," as it was known to its crew, left port to join the U.S. 7th Fleet in the Sea of Japan.[4]

The monthlong voyage gave Dyer plenty of time to acclimate to his new world. Far from the familiar streets of Manchester and his cadre of family and friends, he found himself in a waterborne city of twenty-six hundred souls, all strangers to him. There was no Irish-American Club, no St. Anne's Parish, no band of lifelong chums.

So he kept his head down, did his work, and set about making new friends. And he went to Mass.

There was also training and plenty of it. As a petty officer third class, Dyer was in charge of the weapons on the navy's first carrier-based jets: the Grumman F9F Panthers. The single-engine combat aircraft, the navy's workhorse during the war, carried four 20mm cannons in its nose and rockets and bombs under its wings.[5]

The ship arrived in Japan on June 22,[6] and for the next six months, its planes pounded targets across North Korea, including four major rail centers close to the Soviet and Manchurian borders in the largest air raid of the war at that point,[7] and several hydroelectric power plants near the Chosin Reservoir.[8] The attacks were often met with heavy anti-aircraft fire, and some of Dyer's friends were killed.

But even as he prepped his planes for combat, making sure their ordinance was at its most lethal efficiency, Dyer was beginning to hear another, very different call. In the midst of war, his Roman Catholic faith remained a touchstone in his life. He never missed Mass. And then there was Father Joe. Joseph O'Brien was the Catholic chaplain aboard the *Bon Homme Richard*.

He and Dyer hit it off.

"You have good chaplains and not-so-good chaplains," Dyer recalled. "Father Joe was a good chaplain. He saw himself as a priest, not a chaplain."[9] One day Father Joe stunned the young petty officer when he shouted across the deck, "Dyer, when you get off this ship after the war is over, you're going to seminary!" Dyer fired back, "Father Joe, you better learn how to find your way to a mental hospital after you leave this ship. I'm not going to any seminary."

Undeterred, Father Joe claimed the last word. "Unless you can walk on the Sea of Japan, Dyer, you're mine for the rest of this cruise," he said. "Then let's see what God thinks."[10]

God's thoughts arrived later via a most unlikely messenger.

"Hey, Dyer!"

The sound of his name came floating above the din of sailors on R&R, freed from the tension of combat. The "Bonnie Dick" was in Yokosuka, the U.S. naval base at the entrance to Tokyo Bay and home port of the 7th Fleet. Dyer and his shipmates were doing what sailors do in such circumstances: prowling through the ship's store, looking for ways to spend some of their hard-earned dollars.

"Hey, Dyer!" the voice came again. "I got something for ya!"

This time Dyer looked up. He knew the voice—it was Jim Myers—and he couldn't imagine what Myers might have for him. They were in the same fighter squadron; Myers was a gifted and trusted pilot, but they were not close friends and they were certainly not at all alike.

But here he came, heading straight for Dyer. He was holding a book.

Now Dyer was really puzzled, knowing that Myers's reading tastes ran more toward racy magazines while Dyer was into more serious fare and his beloved mysteries by P.G. Wodehouse and P.D. James. Drawing near, Myers announced proudly—and obviously—"It's a book."

"So it is, Jim, but if it's something you want to read, then I probably don't even want to look at the pictures," Dyer said with a knowing chuckle. Myers replied, "I'd never read this book, but you need to." And he thrust it into Dyer's chest.

Accepting the book in self-defense, Dyer stared dumbfounded at the cover. It was *The Seven Storey Mountain* by Thomas Merton, and it became a key step in the spiritual journey of this young, Catholic petty officer.[11]

It was an example, Dyer would muse many years later, of how the Lord uses all sorts and conditions of men to deliver messages.

It was 1952 and this was Dyer's first encounter with the writings of Merton. First published in 1948 and still a best seller four years later, *The Seven Storey Mountain* was the Trappist monk's autobiographical account of his spiritual journey.

The two men were very different in many ways. Fifteen years older than Dyer, Merton was already a successful author. A graduate of Columbia University with good contacts in New York literary circles, he was well traveled and well read.

Merton spent much of his youth in Europe; Dyer never left Manchester until he joined the navy. Merton's parents were not well off and neither were Dyer's. But a bequest from Merton's grandparents enabled him to live and travel before becoming a monk in a manner Dyer never dreamed of doing. Unlike Dyer, Merton's relationship with his mother was cold and distant.

Religion did not play an important part in Merton's life until he became a Catholic after much soul-searching, while Catholicism was a core belief in Dyer's close-knit family. Dyer volunteered for the navy; Merton declined his brother's entreaties to join the Naval Reserve and was entering a monastery just as his draft board came looking for him in World War II.[12]

But there were also significant similarities between the two. Both came from immigrant families. Both lost a parent at an early age— Merton his mother and Dyer his father. Both loved good books and jazz. And both shared a deep love of the Catholic faith, which nurtured and sustained them.

Most of all, Merton wrote movingly about his love for monastic life—its rhythms, its routines, and its enveloping spirituality. These experiences spoke powerfully to Dyer, and he felt a growing sense of call.

"I read it and said, 'Yeah, I gotta go to a monastery.' "[13]

CHAPTER 3

Set Up by God

It was the nuns. I went up there and saw them living the gospel and I said to myself, this makes sense.[1] —Mark Dyer

Before he heard the call of the monastery, Dyer thought he knew exactly what he wanted to do when he got out of the navy. "I had my mind pretty set that I was going to go to the Columbia School of Journalism," he said, reminiscing long afterward.[2] Dyer loved newspapers, especially *The Boston Globe*, and he was already developing a lucid, engaging writing style that would serve him well over the years. Journalism, it seemed, was a natural choice.

But now he was getting a different message, and it was coming from all directions. "Father Joe was persistent," he recalled. "I was very regular at Mass. If I got killed, I wanted to go to heaven, and Father Joe had something to say to me after every Mass. Our squadron chief petty officer was a Catholic, and if you wanted to get anywhere on the ship, well, they had a lot of power. And our fleet commander was a Catholic. So I was set up by God, really. There was no great fire in the sky, no *basso profundo* 'Come and follow me.' That just wasn't there. But Father Joe was always over my shoulder."[3]

The defining moment came during R&R in Yokohama, when Father Joe took Dyer to visit three nuns who ran an orphanage.

"They were Franciscans—one was Irish, one was French, one was British," Dyer said. "They took care of twelve or thirteen Eurasian-American kids. They had survived World War II and they taught these kids French, English, Japanese, you name it. Any continental language, they knew it. These kids were fluent in multiple languages.

"Father Joe said, 'Look—these nuns suffered through a concentration camp during World War II. That was their dedication to God. Now what are you going to do?'"[4]

That did it.

It was late 1952 and Dyer's enlistment still had two years left, but he began thinking about life after the navy in an entirely different way. "The other guys in the squadron would see me catching up on my Latin," he said, "because in those days [the Catholic liturgy] was all Latin. But in the Roman Catholic Church, where would I go? You have forty or fifty religious orders to choose from. It's like shopping in a store. I wasn't sure where I wanted to go."[5]

The answer, when it came, took him right back to where he started: Manchester, New Hampshire. There, in his hometown, was a Benedictine monastery, Saint Anselm Abbey, which shared a lush, green campus with Saint Anselm College, a Catholic Benedictine liberal arts institution. "For me, the notion of Benedictinism—it is the longest-standing religious order in the Roman Catholic Church—spoke to the genius of Benedict and the Rule of Benedict," Dyer said. Perhaps alluding to what his own experience would be with the order, he added with a smile, "And he was criticized strongly about being liberal."[6]

But Dyer's enlistment wasn't over when the *Bon Homme Richard* returned from Korean waters. He and his squadron were reassigned to another aircraft carrier, the USS *Bennington*, which put to sea on

August 30, 1953, to join ships from eight other NATO nations tak-ing part in Operation Mariner, the largest peacetime naval maneu-ver in history at that time.[7] The *Bennington* spent the remainder of its five-and-a-half-month cruise conducting training exercises while visiting some of the Mediterranean's most picturesque and historic ports, leaving Dyer with a bulging photo album and memories to last a lifetime.

Discharged from the navy on November 18, 1954,[8] he returned to Manchester for a joyous holiday reunion with family and friends. Soon he was set on a course that would take him into the Order of St. Benedict, starting with an undergraduate education at Saint Anselm College.

During that time he spent a year at the American College of the University of Louvain in Belgium, the world's oldest Catholic univer-sity still in existence. In a letter to the novice master of Saint Anselm Abbey, dated December 22, 1958, the rector of the American College, Father Thomas F. Maloney, wrote that Dyer "gave evidence of being a serious student, an obedient seminarian, and a devout young man. At all times he was very generous and cooperative in whatever con-cerned the welfare of the community. He always conducted himself as a well-mannered gentleman."[9]

At Louvain, the curriculum was rigorous, the professors were demanding, and the exams were oral. Once Dyer faced the particu-larly daunting prospect of an oral exam in his Old Testament course taught by renowned scholar Joseph Coppens. "He loved to ask ques-tions about the Bible which were almost impossible," Dyer said. "It was my turn so I went in. He was smoking a cigar and he said, 'I have a historical question for you.' I thought, 'I'm finished, I'm on my way home.'

"Then he started in English—'You're American, right? Can you tell me the development of American jazz in its historic form from the slavery period up through Chicago jazz, and then up to New York and down to bebop?'

"I said to myself, 'Thank you, Jesus,' because my hobby was American jazz. I went on and on and he finally said, 'You are really wonderful on the subject of American jazz.' And I got a high grade."[10]

While at Louvain, Dyer applied himself to other pursuits besides academics, notably skiing and riding a beloved Vespa, the iconic Italian motor scooter that took Europe by storm in the 1950s, which he shared with other students. And he developed a lasting appreciation for Belgian beer. He and his fellow students would also take ski trips by train to Zermatt, Switzerland, at the foot of the Matterhorn, where the train master let them sleep for free in the station loft.

Returning to Manchester, Dyer finished his studies at Saint Anselm College, graduating *magna cum laude* with a bachelor of arts degree in June 1959. Just before graduation, on May 5, 1959, he requested admission to the Novitiate of Saint Anselm Abbey and was accepted.[11]

"He had a beautiful brain, and he was a close friend in our monastery years," recalled the Rev. Peter Guerin, O.S.B., many years later. "Mark and I were in many ways kindred spirits."

Father Guerin was a year ahead of Dyer in the process. Their novice master was the Rev. Christopher Hagen, O.S.B. "We received the same type of monastic formation under Father Hagen," Guerin said. "He had studied at the famous German monastery at Maria Laach in the 1930s. He used to tell us he got the last train out before the Germans took over the monastery. Father Christopher was a very brilliant man—very clear on what he expected of novices. "During his years of formation here, I know [Dyer] was very much in awe—in a good sense of that word—of Father Christopher, who was his mentor in many, many ways."[12]

Fifty years later, the Most Rev. Frank T. Griswold, 25th Presiding Bishop of the Episcopal Church and a contemporary of Dyer, cited Dyer's time at Louvain and in Saint Anselm Abbey as highly influential in his formation as a priest and in his theology. "At Louvain he encountered progressive European Catholicism," Griswold said.

"Also, he had a very ordered theological approach that I think was rooted in his Roman Catholic background. In a sense it reflected the ethos of the Order of St. Benedict. It was very careful, it was not emotional, and it used a gracious language that transcended many of the so-called hot button issues of the day."[13]

In the monastery, Dyer moved through the process in good order, taking his vows as a monk in 1960 and being ordained as a priest on August 25, 1963.[14] Becoming a Benedictine also meant changing his name. "When I took vows as a brother, [the abbot] said 'Give me three names.' I chose Matthew, Matthias, and Mark, and he picked Mark," Dyer said. "He didn't say why."[15]

No matter. Jimmy Dyer was no more, except in family circles, and in his place was Father Mark Dyer. But having just committed to a lifetime of being a Benedictine monk, little did he know that in nine years he would leave Roman Catholicism and join another church in another country.

Yet Dyer did know that he would love monastic life, and he was right. Its simplicity, its sounds, its silences, its holiness, and its abiding sense of community spoke eloquently to him for all of his days.

Awakened at 4:30 a.m. by one of their own ringing a cowbell, the monks were at prayer twenty minutes later. The rest of the day was interspersed with worship, individual and corporate prayer, classes, work, study, meals, and recreation. After evening worship at 7:30 p.m., the balance of the night, reserved for study and prayer, was spent in silence.

Yet within this structure, the monks found plenty of time for humor and laughter. "The monastery is the funniest place in the world," Dyer said. "We were a family of sixty-two people. In the monastery, you think 'Oh, a nice, quiet life,' but you just never knew."[16]

Dyer often told stories about his monastery days. One of his favorites involved a brother who had dementia. He had been cautioned by the abbot to let others answer the doorbell, but he would hurry to the door every time the bell rang nonetheless. Once when he answered the bell, he encountered the nephew of another brother who wanted to tell his uncle that he had gotten married. "What the hell do you want to talk to him about that for?" the monk demanded, before cooler heads intervened. "The young man's uncle was not very pleased, but the rest of us thought it was hilarious," Dyer recalled.[17]

Then there was Brother Bede. A Swiss monk who was the monastery farmer, he believed nothing significant had happened since Benedict died in 547 CE. "He wouldn't even say the rosary because he thought it was just a newfangled thing the nuns were using," Dyer said. On the last day of Brother Bede's life, Dyer was tending to him in the infirmary. "I said, 'Brother Bede, you are going to die and go to heaven today. Is there anything I can do for you?' "

"Now Brother Bede had absolutely no time for piety, none whatsoever," Dyer said, "and earlier that day, a very pious nun had pinned a picture of a bleeding Jesus on his [hospital gown]. So his last request to me was, 'Get that damn Jesus off of me.' "[18]

Dyer's work at the monastery largely involved education. "Our ministry essentially was the academic life,"[19] he said. Dyer was a residence director in one of the Saint Anselm College undergraduate dormitories, and he taught theology. "Mark was the monk proctor in my dorm," recalled the Rev. Mark Cooper, O.S.B., abbot of the monastery in 2015. "I was eighteen years old—a freshman—and Mark lived right across the hall on the first floor.

"What I remember is that he was very good to all of us. He was very prayerful and thoughtful and a good model for young men. . . . It was 1967—we would come out of [our] rooms about 11:00 p.m. and stand around and talk. There was a lot of joking and laughter and he joined in a lot. . . . He would be up and out early to go teach. He was in his room in the evening, often reading. His door was usually open and you could come in to see him. I was very fond of him."[20]

Father Martin Mager, one of Dyer's fellow monks, recalls Dyer as a crackerjack player on the Saint Anselm faculty softball team, which played student teams in intramural tournaments. "The faculty that played on the team was relatively young. We played against mostly college juniors and seniors and they were all in great shape," he recalled. "Mark had a great arm for softball pitching, and wind-ups that were so difficult to do. Nobody could hit him. We did really well, surprisingly well. We won all the games—surprising all the kids. Then we'd always lose one of the final two games and the kids loved that. He was always popular with students. He was a smart, brilliant guy, and it was good for the kids to see him in a different role."[21]

Whenever he could get away from the monastery, Dyer would visit his family's home in Manchester. Each visit meant his favorite foods, starting with his mother's beef stew and biscuits. "And if we knew Uncle Jimmy was coming, we made sure to have fig squares from Freed's Bakery," said his nephew, Jimmy Cashin. "And we would bring him a box of those at Saint Anselm, too."[22] Dyer spent all of his vacations and holidays with his family, recalled his niece, Kathleen Henderson. It was a time of great joy and spiritual enrichment for the young monk.

Recounting his monastery experience in an interview near the end of his life, Dyer said, "In many ways, those were the happiest days of my life. . . . It was so wonderfully human and I miss it almost every day. I really do. The humanity is what I miss—of all those brothers."[23]

CHAPTER 4

Breaking Away

In the monastery there is a wonderful freedom. Evidently
I broke the freedom. I went too far.[1] —Mark Dyer

The winds of change were blowing at gale force in the Roman
Catholic Church and in American society during the 1960s.
They would affect Dyer greatly as he went about his duties as a
newly minted priest.

Pope John XXIII had convened the Second Vatican Council
(informally known as Vatican II) on October 11, 1962, about ten
months before Dyer's ordination. It was a landmark event in the
Catholic Church, the first time its leaders had met to discuss doctrinal issues in nearly one hundred years. More than two thousand
bishops and thousands of others met four times at St. Peter's Basilica
in Rome during the next three years to set a course for the church in
the rapidly modernizing world.

Among other things, Vatican II allowed languages other than
Latin to be used during Mass, permitted Catholics to pray with
other Christian denominations, and encouraged friendship with

non-Christian faiths. While Dyer supported all of these changes, they roiled Roman Catholic waters for some time, generating much dissension, debate, and discussion around him.

Meanwhile, the United States was embroiled in two epic struggles for its moral and social conscience—the civil rights movement and the Vietnam War. Dyer had strong feelings about both—the Benedictine monk embraced the civil rights movement, and the navy combat veteran opposed the Vietnam War. He and the Benedictines found themselves on the front lines of both causes.

The Vietnam War protest movement came to Dyer's doorstep on October 18, 1965, when FBI agents swooped down on Saint Anselm College and arrested David Miller, a young member of the Catholic Worker movement who was distributing anti-war leaflets. Three days earlier, Miller had publicly burned his draft card in New York City, and he became the first person to be prosecuted under a new federal law prohibiting such acts. He was convicted and served twenty-two months in prison.[2]

Passage of the Voting Rights Act in 1965 outlawed discriminatory practices adopted in some southern states after the Civil War and brought hope to many African-Americans who had been denied the right to vote. But on April 4, 1968, the Rev. Dr. Martin Luther King Jr. was fatally shot at the Lorraine Motel in Memphis, Tennessee, giving the civil rights cause its greatest martyr and plunging the nation into paroxysms of grief, anger, and violence. Dyer's abbey dispatched him to attend King's funeral in Atlanta. In a photograph that appeared in newspapers across the country, Dyer was shown with Rabbi Abraham Joshua Heschel, a Polish-born Jewish scholar and civil rights champion who would become a major influence in Dyer's life and theology.

About five months later, as the country's emotions continued to run high over Vietnam, fourteen opponents of the war grabbed headlines in Milwaukee when they used napalm to burn ten thousand draft files. Known as the Milwaukee 14, they were a mixture of laypeople and clergy, including a Benedictine monk named Anthony Mullaney, who taught philosophy at Saint Anselm College.[3]

The trial made a lasting impression on Dyer. Relating the story forty-six years later, he said with pride, "At trial, the judge asked Anthony why they did it and he said, 'We did it because of Jesus Christ. What the federal government is doing is drafting poor people because they have no power. We want to make clear that this is fundamentally wrong.' "[4] Mullaney was sentenced to four years in prison. More than one hundred Saint Anselm students asked the judge to let them serve the jail terms of Mullaney and his companions, but their requests were denied.[5]

There was much ferment on the religious front as well, and Dyer was in the thick of it. Ironically, the Vatican II emphasis on ecumenical and interfaith dialogue and prayer, two areas in which Dyer was already hard at work for the Benedictines, set him on a collision course with the Roman Catholic Church.

"My ministry assignment at the time was ecumenical, and therefore I was rubbing shoulders with the Greek Orthodox and the Russian Orthodox and with Protestants, and it had a sense of transforming me and broadening me," he explained. "One of the things I did—and I thought it was the right thing to do at the time—when you celebrate Mass in the Roman Catholic Church, you pray for the pope. So I prayed for the Archbishop of Canterbury and for the pope of Rome."[6]

That, he said, was the beginning of a journey that took him further and further from the Catholic Church and its doctrine. As he told and retold the story over many years about the circumstances of his final break with the Catholic Church, the details sometimes differed. Many people remember him saying that he was excommunicated because of something he wrote in a doctoral dissertation, a journal article, or some other publication that conflicted with church teaching, and he refused to recant when confronted by Catholic authorities. Dyer told Religion News Service in a 1992 interview that he began moving away from Catholicism when he realized he could not accept the pope's absolute authority because he found no scriptural basis for it.[7]

As the Rev. Dr. Helen Appelberg of Galveston, Texas, remembers it, Dyer told her class at the Seminary of the Southwest in Austin, Texas, in 1990: "I responded to a call to become a Benedictine monk and made my vows to live in a monastery. . . . One day, after having struggled with the deep core of my beliefs and what I could honestly say I believed, I knew I had come to a moment of truth. I went to my prior and bared my soul and told him what I believed and how I came to that and what a struggle it was. We wept together."[8]

In a heartfelt letter dated December 31, 1970, to the Rt. Rev. Gerald F. McCarthy, O.S.B., then the abbot of Saint Anselm Abbey, Dyer appeared to initiate the break with the Catholic Church. While not citing specific doctrinal issues of conflict, he described a long period of soul-searching that led him to the conclusion that he was called by God to make this decision:

> After nearly two and one half years of deep and intense prayer, consultation and suffering, I now feel that before God I must deepen my priestly life and ministry and my life vows to God in a radical change of Christian living. . . . Now I am firmly convinced with God as my judge and Jesus my savior that I must take all the gifts that God has given me at Saint Anselm's and live them as a priest of the Anglican Catholic Communion. I can't in words express the God-given graces, which I believe have led to this decision, but I can tell you that I firmly believe that this choice is a response to God's grace and hence I would sin if I did not respond to it. Once we meet, I will be happy to explain in depth the graces I believe are there. For me, Father, it is deeply a matter of faith—faith in God, His Son, and my priestly ministry. [9]

In that same letter, he also wrote: "I do hope to marry a deeply committed Christian as soon as the Anglican Church would permit it." Naming the woman he married three and a half months later, he added, "I have come to see through prayer and my love for Marie Elizabeth that whatever I criticized at Saint Anselm's was not the fault of you or the community but rather my fault in failing to respond to God's grace here."[10]

No matter what all the reasons were that led to Dyer's leaving the Roman Catholic Church, following through on his intention to join the Anglican Church would have automatically triggered his separation, said the Rev. Mark Cooper, O.S.B., abbot of Saint Anselm Abbey. "Once Father Mark made known his decision to join the Anglican faith, there were immediate excommunication—I know [it's] a very harsh-sounding word, but [it] basically [means] that he was intending to embrace a faith and a state of life not fully compatible with the faith and state of life he was leaving—triggered automatically. It would be the same with me if I made known that I would be attempting marriage or that I was embracing another faith community."[11]

As a student of Dyer's at Virginia Theological Seminary, and later his protégé, the Rt. Rev. Sean Rowe, Episcopal Bishop of Northwestern Pennsylvania, often heard Dyer recount the circumstances of his leaving the Catholic Church. As Rowe recalled, "In my conversations with him, I had the impression that his teaching and writing was beginning to deviate from the church. He was most taken with John Macquarrie [a Scottish-born Anglican priest and theologian] . . . and the more he deviated from [Roman Catholic teaching and doctrine], the more uncomfortable he was there. I think his story is along the lines of others I have heard from those who left religious communities, that he was no longer comfortable with the church's teaching and the community life and he just could no longer live like that."[12]

The Most Rev. Frank T. Griswold offered a similar view: "I know by inference rather than direct discussion that it was far deeper than encountering the Anglican nun who subsequently became his wife. He was at Saint Anselm and I just sense that things became more restrictive and less gracious than the Benedictine ethos he had known there."[13]

Dyer's life changed radically when he left the Catholic Church at the age of forty. "I picked up my few belongings and I walked out into the street. I didn't have two pennies to rub together. I had to start my life all over again," he said.[14]

But not everything changed. Even though he was no longer officially a Benedictine, he kept the name they had given him. "I could have gone back to being James, but [Mark] was who I was," he said.[15]

CHAPTER 5

Charting a New Course

Canadians are great—they don't have all the ecclesiastical folderol that we have. I [was] going to church every Sunday for six or seven or eight weeks. I got to know the rector, and one day he says, "You've been coming to church here, would you like to resume your priesthood?" And I said, "I would love to." He said, "Why don't you take the Wednesday Eucharist? I am an archdeacon in the diocese and I'll fix it with the bishop." Now in the English church, the archdeacon is the one with jurisdiction over priests and parishes. So he had power. He said, "Now you're an Anglican priest." And that was it.[1] —Mark Dyer

The Dyer family took the news hard, but there was no doubt about their loyalty and love. "My mother was very, very strong. She knew her son was right. She said, 'I know my son and I know he is doing the right thing,'" recalled Dyer's sister, Pat.[2]

Kathleen Henderson said his leaving the church caused ripples in the local Catholic community. "A lot of people talked about my uncle, and I know that hurt [his mother], but she would always defend him. She didn't care what other people thought. She had a mind of her own and she just loved him," she said.[3]

Jimmy Cashin recalls his uncle gathering the family together to break the news. There were tears—lots of tears—from everyone, including Dyer. "I remember everybody being in shock. I'm not sure he even gave us a reason for it that day. If he did, I don't remember it. He said, 'The Roman Catholic Church kicked me out and I don't have any place to go and I don't have any money.' " Cashin added, "I remember him saying that he was no longer going to be a Catholic priest or at Saint Anselm. It was very emotional. But he also told us kids that nothing was going to change our relationship with him."[4]

Despite that reassurance, Henderson remembers breaking down. "I was maybe eight or nine. I remember crying because he wasn't going to be near me anymore," she said.[5] Her apprehension was pre-scient. Her uncle was headed for a new job in Canada. "When [I left the monastery], I didn't have any money so a friend got me a job at the University of Ottawa teaching as a lecturer," Dyer said years later.[6]

That was not Dyer's first experience with the Canadian univer-sity. In 1965, sponsored by the Benedictines, he had earned a mas-ter's degree in theology there and a licentiate of sacred theology from Saint Paul University, a Catholic institution affiliated with the University of Ottawa, a public institution. Equipped with these *cum laude* degrees, he taught theology at Saint Anselm College from 1965 to 1970.

Dyer was enrolled as a candidate for a doctor of sacred theology degree, the highest in the pontifical university system of the Catholic Church. But he did not finish his dissertation, the final step toward this degree. During his studies, Dyer was received into the Anglican Church at St. Matthew's Parish in Ottawa in September 1969.[7]

In the fall of 1970, another momentous change was about to occur. Her name was Marie Elizabeth Hamlin. A former nun in the Anglican Order of St. Anne, she had left the order before taking her final vows and was now a student at the University of Ottawa.

She and Dyer met as nun and priest while attending the Ecumenical Conferences of Anglican and Roman Catholic Religious Orders from 1965 to 1969. Dyer was co-chairman of the conference in 1968–69.

"We can't recall our first conversation. It was probably his response to, 'Would you like another cup of tea, Father Mark?'" Marie Elizabeth told Eileen Carey, the wife of former Archbishop of Canterbury George Carey, in her 1998 book, *The Bishop and I*, which explored the lives and roles of the spouses of a number of Anglican bishops. "Mark had been a priest for several years before we met, and I soon realized that his calling was, to him, one of total commitment to God and to preaching and teaching His word. He was and is one of the few holy men I know."[8]

Dyer deeply valued his future wife's spirituality as well. In a December 31, 1970, letter to the abbot of Saint Anselm Abbey, Dyer wrote, "Marie Elizabeth has taught me the meaning of real prayer and real community love and in doing so has taught me the meaning of God."[9]

Born in Johannesburg, South Africa, as Elizabeth Hamlin on May 22, 1932, she went to Boston at the age of twenty-five to pursue her education and teach school. Increasingly called to religious studies and service, she entered the Order of St. Anne, which operated a girls' school in Arlington Heights, Massachusetts, about six miles northwest of Boston. She spent five years there and took the name Marie. After a dispute with the head of school over curriculum, she left at the end of the school year in 1970. At summer's end, she and her mother moved to an apartment in Ottawa because Dyer was there working on a doctoral degree. Marie Elizabeth found work as a substitute teacher, and she and Dyer settled into a courtship that led to an engagement later that year.[10]

"I think it was a very happy time in their life," recalled Victoria Hutchinson, who knew Marie Elizabeth well and visited the couple twice while a freshman at the University of Massachusetts Amherst. "They would go ice skating and get hot chocolate."

Marie Elizabeth had been Hutchinson's English teacher and dorm mother at the Anglican girls' school. "It was a memorable landmark in my life when they told me they were getting married and asked me to be their daughter," said Hutchinson, who later became a dance professor at Salisbury University in Maryland. Hutchinson told them she did not want to be adopted because she had recently been declared as her own legal guardian by the courts and wanted to keep her name, but she said she would gladly consider them to be her parents. "There were about five years when they were Mum and Dad for me," she said. The relationship began a tradition throughout the Dyers' marriage in which their family always included one or more—official or unofficial—foster children.[11]

Marie Elizabeth and Mark were married on April 17, 1971, in Boston. Their wedding was one of two life-changing events for Dyer that year. The other came via a telephone call from the Episcopal Diocese of Massachusetts, where the Rt. Rev. John Melville Burgess had been installed as diocesan bishop on January 17, 1970. The first African-American in the Episcopal Church to head a diocese in the United States, Burgess was building a staff and he wanted Mark Dyer to be a part of it.

Dyer joined Bishop Burgess as missioner to the clergy, or pastor to the pastors, after being received as an Episcopal priest in the United States on June 15, 1971.[12] The New Hampshire native who had left home, country, and Catholicism to chart a new course in life was now back in New England in one of the Episcopal Church's largest and most historic dioceses. Dyer's work was fulfilling—mentoring, counseling, and ministering to 420 diocesan clergy and their families, leading retreats, and providing spiritual direction for Episcopal clergy around the country. He also did some lecturing at General Theological Seminary in New York.

He devoted much of his time and energy to meeting with small groups of diocesan clergy for prayer and Bible study, honing the practice that would be the heart of his ministry to his clergy when he became a bishop. The Rev. Paul Schwenzfeier was in the first clergy group assembled by Dyer in Boston. "We met every two weeks—lunch, theological discussion, Eucharist. There were seven or eight of us who were there every time. It was dramatic—it turned my ministry around," he said.

"You are talking about Mark coming in and really challenging people at the highest level, asking people to share the challenges of their ministry with one another," he continued. "There wasn't anything that wasn't widely shared in our deliberations—marriage, divorce, parish issues, issues in the diocese, the national church. There were times when there were tears, times when there was joy and laughter. What he was trying to do was not just to bring clergy together but to also precipitate their need to come out of isolation. . . . The Lone Ranger mentality had to go out the window if you were going to participate in the way Mark wanted to do things." Schwenzfeier said Dyer had varying degrees of success with the other clergy groups, but the effort overall was "remarkable and transformative in the lives of many of the clergy."[13]

Dyer's efforts were earning him accolades and the respect and admiration of clergy in the Diocese of Massachusetts and beyond. In 1975, at the age of forty-four, Dyer was one of eight people nominated to succeed Bishop Burgess, who was retiring. The voting lasted eight ballots and the eventual winner was the Rev. John B. Coburn, a nationally prominent clergyman and former dean of Episcopal Theological School in Cambridge, Massachusetts.[14] Dyer finished second, but the seeds of his future episcopacy had been sown.

Their personal life was also good for the Dyers. Marie Elizabeth got a job as dorm mother for Massachusetts General Hospital nursing students in a converted hotel near the Boston Common. That added two important contributions to their quality of life: a spacious second-floor apartment to live in and an easy walk to the diocesan office for Mark.

There was time for trips to see the Dyer family in nearby Manchester or at the ocean. There was time for Dyer's niece and nephew, Kathleen and Jimmy, to take the bus from Manchester to visit Uncle Jimmy in the big city. And there was time for Mark and Marie Elizabeth to indulge their passionate loyalties to the Red Sox and the Celtics.

There was also time to start a family. Marie Elizabeth had undergone a hysterectomy while she was a nun, so knowing they would have to adopt, the Dyers turned to Catholic Charities. In the fall of 1972, they adopted a baby and named him Matthew. Five years later, two other children came in quick succession—John at the age of eighteen months in the fall of 1977 and Jennifer as a baby in late 1977.

The arrival of children always brings change, great and small, to the life and rhythm of a family. But for Mark and Marie Elizabeth, the arrival of Matthew brought change, challenges, and encounters with God's all-encompassing love that went far beyond anything they could have imagined.

CHAPTER 6

Matthew

Matthew could do nothing but he could do everything. He was so absolutely helpless—on the living room couch—everybody who visited pretty much genuflected to him. It was really the power of the helpless.[1] —Mark Dyer

Matthew Dyer was born on Friday, September 29, 1972. It was a cool, early fall Boston day punctuated with fog and drizzle. When Mark and Marie Elizabeth brought their baby home, they were full of the excitement and optimism of new parents, imagining the life they would share with their son.

"They came to the house [in Manchester] and rang the doorbell so we could see Matthew. They thought he was in perfect health," said Jimmy Cashin.[2]

Four weeks later on a visit to the pediatrician, the doctor didn't like what he saw. "Something is wrong here," he said. "You better get over to Children's Hospital."[3] The anxious parents hustled their baby boy to the prestigious Boston Children's Hospital, where he underwent a battery of tests. The results were devastating. Matthew had been born with hydrocephalus, or water on the brain, a condition that occurs when fluid builds up within the skull and causes it to swell. And there was more bad news. Matthew had been born with only a brain stem instead of a brain.

"They said, 'Your son doesn't have a brain. He can hear but he doesn't know what he hears. He can see but he doesn't know what he sees,'" Dyer recalled. "Literally, you could shine a flashlight on one side of Matthew's skull and the light would go right through to the other side."[4]

Warning the new parents that their baby would probably not live more than a year—three at the most—sympathetic doctors suggested that he and Marie Elizabeth return Matthew to Catholic Charities in exchange for a healthy child. "Mark went to bed that night in anguish," said the Rev. Dean Borgman, a close friend. "He said, 'If we take that baby back, who in the world will love him the way we do?'"[5]

For the Dyers, the answer was clear, and Marie Elizabeth delivered it in outspoken terms. "It's a good thing that doctor didn't speak Afrikaans [a language of her native South Africa], because my wife gave him a piece of her mind," Dyer said. He added, "We said, 'No, God has given us Matthew and we will care for Matthew.'"[6]

It was a decision that profoundly shaped the rest of their lives. Matthew lived not one year but almost twenty-nine. From crisis and despair came strength and joy. "He outlived his life expectancy over and over and it has affected our ministry. We have had to deal with the range of feelings a handicapped child engenders, as well as many 'theologies' on the will of God," said Marie Elizabeth.[7]

Matthew took up residence on that couch in the living room, where Marie Elizabeth and Mark provided most of his care. Over the years, Matthew's visitors would include parishioners, clergy, friends, neighbors, and world religious leaders. They would sit with him, smile at him, and talk to him.

"Desmond Tutu walked into the house once, and there was Matthew on the couch. Desmond was Desmond and Matthew was Matthew, and that's all there was to it," Dyer said. "Henri Nouwen got very close to Matthew, because he was up in Toronto working with children very much like Matthew."[8] Dyer said that Nouwen, a Dutch Catholic priest, writer, and theologian who spent years living and working with mentally disabled persons, prayed daily for Matthew.

One source of pleasure for Matthew was music, and he reacted joyfully to it, especially anything by Johannes Brahms or Judy Collins. "My wife loved Judy Collins, too, and we went to a concert of hers just outside of Boston. My wife carried Matthew to the concert and we sat out on the lawn in the summer," Dyer recalled. "She said, 'I am going to take him to see her.' I said, 'You'll never get backstage.' Well, she did and she told Matthew's story to Judy Collins, who said, 'Oh, my father was blind, let me hold him.' It was a wonderful moment."[9]

As time passed, the Dyers, still thinking they would have Matthew for only a short while, added John and Jennifer to their family. They all spent the next twenty-four years with Matthew as a central figure in their lives, all the while establishing fierce bonds of love, devotion, admiration, and pride in their older brother.

"Matthew was the most spectacular human I could ever imagine," said John. "I can't explain it—he was just the best. He was my brother. Even though he really didn't understand anything because of his condition, I would try to know what he was thinking and how he was feeling. I would try to get some of his brain waves going and talk to him."[10]

"Matthew was an incredible blessing. He was the sweetest thing—helpless—but he was always there as a force. He was such a force," said Jennifer. "Mom and Dad and John and I all shared in feeding him and giving him bottles, helping with the laundry, changing his diapers, and giving him baths at the sink. Basically Matthew was the focal point of our home and our family. You ask what we did as a family—Matthew was the central focus and main consideration."

She added, "I just felt so lucky knowing how much light and love and basically pure innocence he radiated in the center of our family. He didn't have the complications of someone with an ego or a mind to think and worry about things. But he did have feelings. He had fear, he cried, he felt pain, and he felt joy and happiness—the basic states. And we all felt so sad when he was in pain and suffering and crying. And we loved to make him laugh, especially John and Dad."[11]

"How he [Mark] loved Matthew," said Kathleen Henderson. "He was so good to Matthew. To see the two of them—he and Marie Elizabeth—with Matthew, it was so amazing."[12]

Often calling Matthew "my spiritual director," Dyer prized the time he spent with his oldest son as one of life's great blessings. "Matthew was a spiritual center for him," said Borgman. "When he was with Matthew, it was a quiet, centering time. He could just be because Matthew just loved.

"I think, too, that his life with Marie Elizabeth and Matthew was a powerful example of grace. He was exhibiting, he was preaching, he was illustrating the grand mystery of the Incarnation, about God in the form of Jesus being willing to waste time with ordinary people.

"Mark related how he would come in from work and sit on the couch and give a little whistle through his teeth, at which Matthew would break out into a little smile. He would just sit there, stroking his son, with whom no other communication was possible. 'That's what God has done for us,' Mark would say. 'All I can do with this son of mine is waste time with him. In similar fashion, the Son of God has interrupted eternal glory to waste time with a beggar, a blind man, a desperate woman—with all of us.' "[13]

The Very Rev. Martha J. Horne, dean and president of Virginia Theological Seminary from 1994 to 2007 and a friend and colleague of Dyer, said, "Matthew taught him a lot about dependence and not being anxious about it. . . . Matthew gave him a gift—his presence."[14]

Another colleague said, "Mark always said that no matter what the day had been like, Matthew was the centerpiece."

Marie Elizabeth applied the full force of her considerable will to advocating for Matthew and fighting his battles. "She was this powerful, almost irrational defender of Matthew. They were told Matthew probably would only live three months but at the very most three years," said Borgman. "When she would take Matthew for a tooth problem or other physical problem . . . she would fight tenaciously for that boy's life. The fact that he outlived her is one of life's tragic ironies."[15]

CHAPTER 7

Rector

Now I tend to be somewhat radical, and the Wednesday before the first Sunday when I celebrated the Eucharist, I took all the flags, including the American flag, out of the church. On Sunday I am standing at the door of the church after the service, and here comes George Patton [son and namesake of the famed World War II general]. I had never met him and he had never met me. I was a navy petty officer and he was a major general. He said, "Where are the blankety-blank flags?" I said, "George, let's get one thing straight right now. There's only one commander-in-chief inside that door—his name is Jesus Christ and that's that." He looked at me and said, "You know, that's right, isn't it?"[1] —Mark Dyer

S o began Dyer's tenure as rector of Christ Church in Hamilton, Massachusetts.

It was 1978, the year he turned forty-eight, and Dyer was fresh off a stint as priest-in-charge at embattled Trinity Church in Bridgewater, Massachusetts. He had been dispatched there in late

1976 by Bishop Coburn after the rector and many communicants left
the Episcopal Church ("taking the building with them") following
that year's General Convention, which approved the ordination of
women and declared that "homosexual persons are children of God
who have a full and equal claim with all other persons upon the love,
acceptance, and pastoral concern and care of the Church."[2]

Founded in 1747, Trinity was one of the oldest parishes in one
of the Episcopal Church's oldest dioceses. But it was facing an existential crisis. Performing pastoral triage, Dyer quickly rallied the
few remaining faithful and recruited new members as the parishioners began meeting in a Congregational church, later moving to
a Methodist church.[3] The experience tempered him for challenges
that lay ahead.

With that experience under his belt and a near miss at being
elected bishop of the Diocese of Massachusetts in 1975, Dyer seemed
a likely candidate to become a rector. Christ Church of Hamilton and
Wenham, a moneyed parish on Boston's North Shore, came calling.

David Bergquist, a parish member and lay leader for more than
forty years, remembered Dyer's arrival. "The rumor was spread
about—and I think there was some validity to it—that having lost
in an election for bishop in one race, the prospect of being called
on another occasion down the road was, in all likelihood, a given,"
he said. "And the one strike against him to a certain extent was that
he had not been a rector. So they felt that he needed a parish on the
résumé as a rector to just sort of close the loop. And so we were that
experience that needed to be had, so to speak. But we were happy
to have the opportunity to be his flock. It wasn't as if we felt that we
were being used for some other purpose."[4]

Though scarcely fifty miles apart, Christ Church in Hamilton
and Trinity Church in Bridgewater were in different worlds. Twenty-
five miles south of Boston, Bridgewater was a working-class town of
about twenty-six thousand known for its ironworks, a state prison,
and a state university. Thirty miles north of Boston, Hamilton was

a town of about seventy-five hundred with no industry or any land even zoned for industry. The town included South Hamilton and it bordered its neighbor to the south, Wenham. Settled in 1638 and named for Alexander Hamilton, whose portrait adorns the town seal, Hamilton lay in a bucolic land of country estates, tree-lined lanes, and a rich equestrian heritage where polo was played on Sundays.[5]

Despite the town's lengthy history, the Episcopal Church was a relative newcomer there. Hamilton was a bastion of the Congregationalist Church, and church government and town government were not separated until 1829. The railroad came in 1839, followed by the Methodists in 1859. But it was not until 1912 that a group of women petitioned the Episcopal bishop to establish a parish there.[6] Fifteen years later, on Easter Sunday, the first Christ Church building was dedicated.[7] The area was home to many prominent New England families, including that of General Patton. Patton Park in Hamilton is named for the general and features a Sherman tank, one of the kind on which he made his reputation as the hard charging armored commander known as "Old Blood and Guts."

Members of those families populated the pews of Christ Church and underwrote its operations with substantial checks. Dyer referred to them as "noble Republicans" and "the financial bulls of Christ Church." He had never encountered such a concentration of wealth, status, and influence. "They could touch wood and it would become money," he said. "When I got there, I was told that if I ever needed money for the church, all I had to do was make a phone call. That was it." On the spiritual side of the ledger, Dyer said, "They had a very strong sense of Catholic Christianity. That's why I was called."[8]

"When Mark arrived, things really started happening from the get-go of a very positive nature," Bergquist recalled.[9] It wasn't that Christ Church needed a jump start. It had been on a growth spurt and was the third largest church in the Diocese of Massachusetts, with more than five hundred people in church on Sundays. Dyer wanted to concentrate on the spiritual side of things, as he would throughout his ministry, and he had his own vision of "Catholic Christianity."

"The first thing he did that I remember was changing the celebration of the Eucharist to every Sunday morning at every service. We had been doing the Eucharist alternatively during the month— two weeks of Morning Prayer, two weeks of Eucharist," Bergquist said. "Change is always one of those things that creates waves—and a lot of people thought something Anglican was being lost by this [even though the change was called for in the revised Episcopal Book of Common Prayer issued in 1979] and we were becoming more Catholic because he was a former Catholic priest."[10]

More changes were coming. Dyer instituted a system of small group meetings in people's homes for Bible study, prayer, and fellowship. He introduced new services to the parish—midweek Eucharist, healing services, daily morning and evening prayer, and the Easter Vigil. A member of the vestry said they ought to be praying regularly for every member of the parish, so they created a parish-wide prayer list and did exactly that. Through it all, Dyer constantly called his flock to a disciplined prayer life buttressed by daily reading of scripture.

"Prayer was so important to him," Bergquist said. "In fact, his last sermon here was on the Lord's Prayer. I remember him introducing it by saying, 'If I have left you with nothing else, I hope it is my concern for prayer in the life of an individual Christian and in the body of Christ.' He really expected people to develop a rather intense prayer life and a sense of spirituality.

"For example, in his rector's report of 1981—midstream in his time here—he wrote, 'I offer a call to personal holiness through the power of the Holy Spirit in Christ.' In other words, he was not laying out a programmatic agenda—he was asking people to ramp up their spiritual life. . . .

"I think Mark left an indelible mark on the people who were here to feel that way about their faith. I saw where someone said in this age of CEO bishops, he was a totally different kind of person—and I mean that from a spiritual perspective. Mark talked about making Jesus Christ the center of your life, and he exhibited that in his own life."[11]

"Mark was a unifier," said the Rev. Dean Borgman, who served as a longtime assistant in the parish. "We are a church of professors, artists, intellectuals, and writers, and he could come into that church and feel [at home]. He had that ecumenical desire and gift that brought people together. When he talked to a person, it was a special spiritual event. . . . I think he had that gift of making ordinary people feel special. I think it's a wonderful gift when a priest can make people feel very special in our Lord."[12]

Diana Butler Bass, an Episcopal layperson, writer, and teacher, attended Christ Church while Dyer was rector. In her book, *Strength for the Journey: A Pilgrimage of Faith in Community*, an account of her experiences in eight Episcopal churches, she wrote: "Until I went to Christ Church, I do not think I ever heard the word *spirituality* used in a positive sense. . . . But Mark Dyer introduced this word into my world and into the world of the evangelicals of South Hamilton."[13]

Bass was in South Hamilton attending Gordon-Conwell Theological Seminary, an evangelical Protestant institution. Dyer had begun teaching there and students packed his courses on early Christian history and medieval spirituality. Many also began attending Christ Church. "A good number of non-Episcopalians—particularly the Presbyterians—were attracted to his vision of a monastic-type spirituality that combined a love of learning and the desire for God," she wrote. "Despite the denominational differences, they thronged to Christ Church to sit under him and be mentored in liturgical worship and medieval spirituality."[14] Dyer's "Benedictine-tinctured Anglicanism," Bass stated, "meshed with their spiritual longings."[15]

Soon after arriving, Dyer went looking for a new assistant. He found what he was looking for in Titus Presler, who came with glowing recommendations from General Theological Seminary. The Harvard-educated Presler, who was from the Diocese of Massachusetts, had studied for two years at Gordon-Conwell before transferring to General, so he already knew the area. He had also heard Dyer speak and came away "inspired and deeply impressed." When Presler saw the opening for a curate at Christ Church, he applied immediately and was invited for an interview.

Presler and his wife drove up the New England coast on a cloudy, chilly spring day to meet Dyer at Woodman's Clam Shack, a venerable seaside eatery in Essex, Massachusetts. "I could barely hope that I could have the opportunity to work with Mark Dyer, such was my high regard for him," said Presler. Yet to his amazement, while they communed over fried clams, Dyer was more intent on persuading Presler to come to Christ Church than on grilling him about his qualifications. "I was just dumbfounded by that," Presler recalled. "I don't recall him asking much at all about my experience or my sense of the church or anything like that."[16]

Suffice it to say, the interview went well and Presler found himself at Christ Church by August 1979. He would be the only full-time clergy assistant while Dyer was rector. Despite Presler's lack of experience, Dyer treated him as a full partner in ministry, and the new curate's evangelical credentials helped him build bridges to that part of the Christ Church congregation.

Presler also had a front row seat to observe Dyer's unique approach to ministry, which he would later employ on a larger scale as a bishop. At Christ Church, Dyer largely relied on lay leaders to handle the business and administrative affairs of the church while he focused predominately on spiritual matters. Dyer had a light touch with staff, meeting individually with people as needed but never conducting staff meetings.

After a year or so, Presler went to Dyer to find out how he was doing as a new priest. "He looked at me and paused a moment and thought and he said, 'You've been faithful.' And that was it," Presler said decades later, the recollection of the exchange with his mentor bringing him to the brink of tears. "I had expected we would go down a checklist, but I treasured that one sentence and I realized how much was rolled into that one sentence. And I realized that in a way, that was the highest thing Mark could say, because his view of ministry was about faithfulness. So if one has been faithful, that's all one needs to be."[17]

Presler, who later became president of the Seminary of the Southwest and academic dean at General Theological Seminary, said many years later that in retrospect, Dyer's spiritual leadership as rector was a great strength but his lack of collaboration and direction of staff was a weakness. Dyer extended his spiritual approach to the conduct of church business, changing vestry meetings in form and substance. Meetings now began with Eucharist. He asked the senior warden to lead the meetings, emphasizing the role of lay leadership and allowing Dyer to be more involved in discussions. And he introduced a new approach to decision-making that emphasized discernment.

"Mark felt very strongly about unanimity of decision-making on the vestry," Bergquist said. "In other words, every vestry vote or decision had to be a unanimous one. A lot of people felt this was virtually idealistic and an impossibility to achieve . . . but he really pursued that because he thought it was very biblical and theologically sound. And eventually it was attained. But it was short-lived, because once he left, that whole principle began to sort of just die a natural death."[18]

Even with his strong emphasis on spiritual stewardship, Dyer did not neglect fiscal stewardship. Despite the wealth of many of its parishioners, Christ Church had little if any endowment in those days and it had a growing physical plant to take care of.

A second church building had been constructed in 1962. It seated more than 350 and the 1927 building, seating 144, had become the chapel. Both had handsome exteriors of local fieldstone, but the new

church boasted an expansive, modern sanctuary and included striking stained glass windows, both twentieth-century American and
thirteenth-century French.[19] "It is the most beautiful church I have
ever celebrated in," Dyer said. "I so loved that church and the people."[20]

In Dyer's second year as rector, Christ Church launched Renewal
'79, a capital campaign aimed at putting the parish on a more solid
financial footing. The campaign raised about $250,000 to begin an
endowment that later exceeded $1.5 million. "Mark was instrumen-
tal in a lot of heavy lifting in getting people to give to the parish at
that time," Bergquist said. "We always think of him as a spiritual
person, above the fray, but he was very important in the life of the
parish in terms of the financial approach that we took."[21]

Renewal '79 had a major impact on another one of Dyer's top
priorities: mission work. Christ Church had a strong commitment
to mission before Dyer arrived, and with endowment income now
going toward maintenance of church buildings, the church could
earmark half of its annual operating budget for mission projects,
both foreign and domestic. Christ Church had already established
a South American Missionary Society, which sent people to live and
serve in those countries for two or three years. In 1979, the church
also raised $5,000 for Cambodian refugees.[22]

Another idea for a local mission project brought Christ Church
together with a very different parish in a unique partnership. "Mark
was very close personal friends with Paul Schwenzfeier, who was the
rector of the Church of the Holy Spirit in Mattapan, an inner-city
Boston parish that had a lot of immigrants in its population, most
notably Haitians," said Bergquist.[23]

Dyer and Schwenzfeier, who met in Boston while Dyer was
on Bishop John Burgess's staff, set about developing a relationship
between the wealthy, white suburban parish and its edgier, diverse,
urban counterpart, where parishioners from thirty-seven nations
spoke seven languages. Schwenzfeier said he insisted on two conditions: first, it had to be a genuine two-way relationship involving

parishioners of both churches and not just Christ Church sending money to his parish; and second, Christ Church members had to be willing to come to Mattapan regularly.

"It was never great numbers of people but they understood the need to visit, and they tried to set up a scheme [where] people would come at least once a month," Schwenzfeier said. "Nonetheless there was a lot of good that came from the relationship . . . and some members of Christ Church even joined our congregation."[24]

Then came a foreign mission opportunity that provided one of the most formative experiences of Dyer's ministry. In the summer of 1981, he led a group of Gordon-Conwell graduate students to the Mother House of Mother Teresa's Missionaries of Charity in Calcutta. They worked side by side with the nuns during the day, tending the dying and destitute. At night, Dyer taught classes for his students and for novices of the order. He spoke reverently about that time for the rest of his life.

"When I was there [in Calcutta], there had been a massive spread of leprosy on the street and we managed to figure out there were probably thirty-five thousand active street lepers in the city of Calcutta at that time. And so, we went out with the sisters to the clinics and the street, to bind up their wounds, to give whatever drugs we could administer, and just to help people, knowing that they would still be on the street and it would be almost impossible to contain the growth of their leprosy.

"One day, as a man was standing in line waiting for pills, he came up to me and he said, 'Father, would you lay hands on my head and pray for me?' His leprosy was very active; his face was disfigured, he had lost his ears and just looked terrible and scared the daylights out of me. 'Would you lay hands on me and pray for me?' he said. Well, having grown up in the proper way, I went to the sister for an answer.

"I went to Sister Shanti, herself a physician, a nun, and an expert in leprosy, so I thought I was in good hands. I said, 'Sister Shanti, he wants me to lay hands on his disfigured head and pray for him, and he has active leprosy. What am I to do?' And she looked me straight in the eyes and she said, 'What would Jesus do, Father?'

"I said, 'I want a clinical opinion now, Sister.' She said, 'You won't get one from me.' And I entered the world of the handicapped in a very powerful and wonderful way."[25]

Back at home, Mark and Marie Elizabeth settled into a lifestyle of work and family the likes of which Christ Church had never seen. They set up house with Matthew, Jennifer, and John in the rectory, a roomy two-story house with a mansard roof built on the church grounds in 1951. "Matthew would always be on the couch in the living room," recalled Dean Borgman. "The rectory was always open. I don't think that rectory has been so open since with people just dropping in. . . . That openness and vulnerability and compassion were on display for the congregation."[26]

"Marie Elizabeth carried Matthew almost everywhere she went around here. They were literally almost linked at the hip," said Bergquist. "It was a kind of curiosity for us to have such a couple in our midst who were so atypical of the kind of people we more or less were accustomed to encountering in those roles. In other words, there was no blueprint here. In came Mark, a former Roman Catholic priest—not advanced in years but a little bit—and Marie Elizabeth, who was distinctly South African, with that edge that I think goes with being British to a certain extent.

"She was not mannerless but very much to the point—never talked around an issue but got right to the heart of it. . . . I think a lot of people saw her as a sort of supernumerary to Mark's ministry. There was a certain duality to it. There was a feeling they were very linked up in the life of the parish. She was not seen as the wife of the rector who serves tea."[27]

"Marie Elizabeth was fiery, opinionated—strong yet very compassionate," said Dean Borgman's wife, Gail, also a close friend of the Dyers. "There was this intensity about Marie Elizabeth—like she was running on coffee and cigarettes, even though she didn't smoke. Mark had a wonderful way of covering the blister of Marie Elizabeth. She would come out with something and he would just say 'What?' and then he would smile. But they gave each other a lot of room to preserve and practice their gifts."[28]

Meanwhile, both were growing and changing in their callings. Dyer still felt a trace of bitterness over his loss to John Coburn in the election to become bishop of the Diocese of Massachusetts, Presler said, and he mused from time to time about the prospect of becoming a bishop somewhere else. "I remember Mark saying to me at one point, 'Here at Christ Church I have my own diocese,'" recalled Presler, saying that Dyer had pointed with pride to his thriving parish. "I could well understand his feeling."[29]

Opportunity next knocked in November 1980 when Dyer was nominated to become bishop coadjutor of the Diocese of Central New York, which stretches from Canada to Pennsylvania and includes Syracuse. He was not selected but his candidacy enhanced his reputation outside his own diocese.[30]

There was a growing demand for Dyer's services as a preacher and retreat leader, and he took on more work for the Diocese of Massachusetts. As a result, Dyer began to spend more time away from the parish, and there were some rumblings of discontent. His Irish temper, usually kept well under wraps, would occasionally flare. "I heard him say once, 'If they think that I'm just going to be a quiet, stick-at-home country parish rector, they made a big mistake,'" recalled Bergquist. "But I think overall, this parish had a self-image that they wanted a certain cachet—we've got Mark Dyer and we're booming."[31]

With the doors of the Episcopal Church swinging open to allow the ordination of women, Marie Elizabeth embarked on that journey, becoming a deacon in 1979 and a priest in 1980. She began work as a chaplain at Children's Hospital in Boston, but did not join the clergy staff at Christ Church.[32]

There was considerable opposition in the Christ Church congregation to the notion of women priests, and Marie Elizabeth took an uncharacteristically low profile on the subject. "Even though Marie Elizabeth Dyer was a priest and would later be quite successful in her ministry, she was so low-key at Christ Church that she was almost invisible," Diana Butler Bass wrote.[33]

Even so, there was growing unease at Christ Church, as there was at many Episcopal churches at that time, as American societal norms underwent rapid change. The denomination's new positions on women's ordination and the acceptance of homosexuals—not to mention the introduction of the 1979 prayer book—left many Episcopalians feeling uncomfortable with the changes taking place in what had been their mainstream, established denomination.

Even more changes were in store for the Dyers.

CHAPTER 8

Bishop

I was driving on Route 20, and there were three trucks in front of me going up a long hill at five miles an hour. One car comes right up behind me and then passes. Then another. Then another. Then another. So I pass, too, but when I get up to the top of the hill, those four cars are lined up by a state trooper, and he waves me over, too. I quickly buttoned up my bishop's shirt and said to myself, "I gotta look at the name tag on this guy's shirt." I looked and his name was Polish and I thought, "I've got it made. I'm not gonna get fined here today."

So I rolled the window down, and he looks in and I started out like a good, old-fashioned Catholic—"Bless me, Officer, for I have sinned. It's been seven months since my last confession." He said, "You are something else. You are very fortunate today. The other four drivers in front of you don't want to go to confession. Now, get out of here, Father." I tell you, I had more fun in that job.[1] —Mark Dyer

Mark Dyer was stunned. Someone—he didn't know who—had put up his name as a candidate to become bishop coadjutor of the Diocese of Bethlehem, Pennsylvania. He hadn't sought the job. He couldn't find the place without a map. And yet, the more he thought about it and prayed about it, the more he discerned a strong sense of call—not to mention fit.

The Episcopal Diocese of Bethlehem covered fourteen counties in northeastern Pennsylvania, lying north and west of Philadelphia. It included all of the Lehigh Valley and cities like Allentown, Reading, Scranton, and Wilkes Barre. In the shadow of two of the major urban centers on the East Coast—New York is a two-hour bus ride away—it is nonetheless in a world of its own. Bisected diagonally by ridges of the Appalachian Mountains, the diocese overlies belts of anthracite coal and slate in its northern and western regions. These rich deposits fueled a mining industry that in turn fed steel mills to the south. The city of Bethlehem, with a population of about seventy thousand, was home to the Bethlehem Steel Corporation, at that time the second-largest steel producer in the United States.

The mix of mining and manufacturing had engendered a strong work ethic, fostered some of the same fierce feelings of pride and self-reliance, and established the same bedrock values built on family, religion, and hard work that surrounded Dyer as he grew up in working-class Manchester, New Hampshire. These were his kind of people and he instinctively understood them and could connect with them on matters of faith and family.

But their way of life was under assault by the time Dyer arrived in 1982. Economic fortunes had changed. Mines were closing and steel plants were laying off workers. Jobs that had been secure for generations were vanishing. "The diocese started north of the Main Line outside of Philadelphia, but the further north it went, the poorer it got. There were abandoned coal mines and men with black lung disease," Dyer recalled.[2]

That same year, Billy Joel released his song "Allentown," named for Bethlehem's neighboring city, which described the factory closings and unemployment lines that were commonplace in both towns when Dyer arrived.[3] "Billy Joel got it right, you know," Dyer, ever the music buff, would say many times over the years as he recited the lyrics. "He really did."[4]

Bishop Lloyd E. Gressle, who had served since 1971, was retiring at the end of 1983, and the diocese was looking for a successor to come in a year earlier to provide for a smooth transition. There were five candidates for the position, but Dyer stood out and was elected on the third ballot by clergy and lay delegates to the diocesan convention.

"What sold the deal was his spirituality and Mark's role as pastor to the clergy of the Diocese of Massachusetts," said the Ven. Richard I. Cluett, a member of the search committee. "The clergy here were hungry for someone who would come in and nurture their spirituality. The clarity and depth of his faith was evident, as was his ability to talk about it, share it, and live it. And he already had a track record with the clergy of the Diocese of Massachusetts doing exactly that."[5]

Dyer's Roman Catholic background also served him well as a potential pastor for the fourteen thousand Episcopalians in the diocese. "The ethos of the diocese is Catholic," said Jim Naughton, an Akron, Ohio–based church communications consultant who grew up in Scranton as a Roman Catholic. "It is swimming in Catholic waters. I think as a result of that, Mark's Catholic background made him distinctly qualified to bring what was the culture of the area into the Episcopal Church, but to do it in a way that was informed by his own journey.

"There were also a lot of Vatican II Catholics who felt that Vatican II had run out of steam. Mark, in some ways, was a good shepherd for those kinds of folks. But on top of that, as learned and pastoral as he was, I think those gifts were really well-matched with the Episcopal Church in that area."[6]

Dyer accepted the call, and he and Marie Elizabeth moved to Bethlehem with Jennifer, John, and Matthew. He was consecrated as bishop coadjutor on November 6, 1982, and became the diocesan bishop on December 3, 1983.

Not only did the Diocese of Bethlehem have a new bishop, but the new bishop had a very new way of doing things. Actually, it was a very old way of doing things—the Benedictine Way. Formed by his years as a monk, Dyer organized his episcopate on the monastic structure of abbot and prior. Dyer would be the abbot, or the chief spiritual officer of the diocese, rather than the chief executive officer. As he spelled out in a detailed plan, he would have few if any administrative duties, devoting his time instead to serving as pastor to the clergy, focusing on their spiritual health and well-being as the key to developing spiritually healthy congregations. He would also be a constant presence for the people in his sixty-eight parishes.

The job description Dyer wrote for himself called for him to "pray without ceasing, personally and daily at Diocesan House with all staff for needs and parishes of the diocese"; meet twice monthly with his priests for prayer, Bible study, and pastoral care; visit every parish at least every eighteen months; and provide a "vision of the church" through an annual address at the diocesan convention and six annual pastoral letters. Dyer's plan also called for sharing "ministry of the Episcopate with staff by delegation of responsibility and authority in all other areas."[7] He quickly set about assembling a staff that could thrive in such an environment.

The Rev. Robert Rowley Jr., a retired navy captain and judge advocate, was called first as canon to the ordinary, or diocesan administrator. Next came Cluett as archdeacon to work with clergy and congregations. Cluett knew the diocese and community well, having served as a rector since 1978, and before that as a community organizer for the U.S. Office of Economic Opportunity. When Rowley left in 1989 to become bishop coadjutor of the neighboring diocese of Northwestern Pennsylvania, Cluett assumed responsibility for staff oversight and day-to-day administration, becoming the prior while Dyer functioned as abbot.

For his canon theologian and communication minister, Dyer reached into the ranks of fellow ex-Roman Catholic priests and tapped former Monsignor Bill Lewellis. Kindred spirits with a shared theological formation, they would collaborate on many writing projects. Lewellis also cultivated valuable relationships with the press, and he ran an independent, award-winning diocesan newspaper.

The Rev. T. Scott Allen arrived in 1989 as social missioner. He would spearhead many of Dyer's initiatives in mission work—as had Social Missioner Sue Cox before Allen—which galvanized local parishes with a renewed sense of purpose and won national recognition. His portfolio also included HIV/AIDS ministry, anti-racism work, and ecumenical relations.

In working with his staff, Dyer lived up to the spirit and letter of his operational plan. Lewellis experienced the difference immediately when he joined Dyer after serving in a similar position in the Catholic Diocese of Allentown. "The unwritten job description there was 'Be safe, be right, promote the institution.' Mark's expectations were 'Take risks, though you may fail, be creative, and promote the gospel,'" Lewellis said.[8]

"He delegated everything except spiritual matters and religious decisions. Each staff member had full responsibility and authority in their area. They wouldn't have to come to him for permission," Cluett said. "He would not ask people about what they were working on, what they were doing. His expectation was that if you needed him, you would come to him."

As for Dyer's role, "He saw himself as the abbot of a religious community, a spiritual guide, leader, and teacher," Cluett explained. "He understood his role as 'focusing God for the people of God.' His primary vehicle for doing that was working with the clergy."

And his primary vehicle for working with the clergy was his Dodge Caravan. "He was the first bishop I knew who drove around in a big van," Cluett said. "They had it so they could haul the kids and Matthew around."[9]

Every week, usually on Tuesdays and Thursdays, Dyer would hit the road for face-to-face sessions with his clergy in six regional groups throughout the diocese. "I would ask during those visits, 'What is the scripture telling us?' We would pray and we would study the scripture together," Dyer said.[10] The readings were always those for the following Sunday, so the study sessions aided sermon preparation while enhancing general scriptural knowledge.

Between those twice-monthly meetings and his visits to the parishes, the circuit-riding bishop logged thirty-five thousand miles a year in his van and soon became a familiar sight to his flock. "His ministry was working with the spiritual development of the clergy and providing pastoral support of the clergy. The only reason he was able to do this was because of the abbot and prior model," Cluett said. "It was hugely important in terms of demonstrating the bishop's office's commitment to [the] congregations and their well-being to spend all his time doing that. Not only that, if I am the rector in Tamaqua and I have something I want to get off my chest, I don't have to drive three and a half hours to see the bishop because I know I am going to see him in two weeks max."[11]

Dyer's approach to spirituality and the experience of those Bible study sessions made lasting impressions on many clergy, including other bishops who heard about what Dyer was doing and came to see for themselves. Dyer's methods especially inspired a young priest named Anthony R. Pompa, who later became dean and rector of the Cathedral Church of the Nativity in Bethlehem. "I can't stress enough what it was like to swim in the waters of this diocese at that time, which was saturated with his leadership, which was the Benedictine Way," Pompa said. "It was affirming, it was spirit-driven, it was scripturally saturated, and it was open to the Spirit in a lovely, lively, beautiful way for a young kid from the coal regions who didn't know squat."

But this positive assessment of the Dyer-led scripture study sessions was not unanimous among diocesan clergy. "In hindsight,"

Pompa said, "I will hear from some people who were there then who say, 'Well, we really didn't have much interaction; it was kind of like Mark holding court.' Well, yes, it was Mark holding court, but he was great. He could hold court at any time and that was fine with me. But you know how it goes—you get a bunch of clergy in a room and we all think we can do it better."[12]

Priorities and Passions

Dyer arrived at his new post to find that he had no home and no office. The former diocesan headquarters several blocks away, a rambling, mostly empty structure that had once housed seminarians, had been sold, along with Bishop Gressle's home next door. So, after getting a loan from a clergy assistance fund to buy a house, Dyer set up an office in the cathedral basement and got to work. The new bishop embraced his role with zest, humility, and his deep sense of spirituality, which permeated the tone and priorities of the diocesan staff and even the physical layout of the diocesan headquarters.

When he became diocesan bishop, he moved immediately to convene a conference on spirituality and mission in January 1984. "He said we had an annual convention for the business of the church, and we needed a spirituality and mission conference for the real business of the church," Lewellis recalled.[13]

As plans emerged to renovate and combine two rundown row houses for diocesan offices, Dyer insisted on a light-filled, airy worship space in the center with striking stained glass windows. The space was behind a small entryway and reception area and was the first thing any visitor would see. The diocesan staff met for worship there at 8:30 a.m. every workday, rotating responsibilities for leading the service—Morning Prayer on Monday through Thursday and Eucharist on Friday, followed by a staff meeting.

"I think life at home was pretty hectic in the mornings getting the kids up and ready for school, so I don't know how much time he had for prayer there in the mornings," Cluett said. "But he would come in here and have Morning Prayer every morning. Then, sometimes he would just go upstairs, close his door, and take care of his faith. When he was here, he was very much like Brother Lawrence [a seventeenth-century Carmelite lay brother in France]—a walking prayer. That certainly was his definition for how he approached what he did."[14]

There was also much room for humor, spirited conversations around the office coffee pot, and passionate discourses about the fortunes of Dyer's beloved Boston Red Sox. "I loved going to work, I really did. I remember going to work and just howling with laughter," Dyer said. "In many ways, these were the best years of my life."[15]

But all was not fun and games. Lewellis vividly remembers a coffee pot conversation with Dyer in January 1986 when the bishop seemed uncharacteristically glum. He had met the night before with a committee of mostly wealthy men who convened at a country club to set the diocesan operating budget. By tradition, money for operations came from mandatory parish assessments while money for mission and other ministries came from voluntary contributions.

Dyer was determined that system had to change. "If people expect me to lead this diocese by the bottom line, I'll go back to Boston and drive a cab," he growled to Lewellis.[16]

The system changed.

Soft-spoken and gentle, with a ready smile and a trademark twinkle in his eye, Dyer seldom showed signs of anger. But an Irish temper dwelled within, and it flared on occasion. "He got angry rarely but it was a rich, Irish anger when it rose up," Cluett said. "I never heard him raise his voice. When he got angry, his pale face would redden, his eyes would lose their glint, and his voice would harden and become very firm as he addressed a person. It was almost always over what he deemed to be an injustice being done toward someone."[17]

Adding to his portfolio while bishop, Dyer undertook several important assignments for the Episcopal Church. In 1983, he joined the third round of talks between the Episcopalians and the Lutherans as they continued decades of dialogue gradually moving them toward an alliance, which was achieved in 2000.

In 1992, Dyer was one of three bishops in a delegation of eight Americans who traveled to Moscow to meet with their counterparts in the Russian Orthodox Church and discuss the role of bishops. With the fall of communism and the collapse of the Soviet Union at the end of 1991, restrictions on religious freedom and church activities had been lifted. But the new government, known as the Russian Federation, was struggling to find its way in the new political and economic order, as was the church, which was looking to establish its role in providing spiritual and moral leadership. The talks, which covered topics ranging from theology to church structure and governance, took place at St. Daniel Monastery in Moscow from June 22–27, and Dyer delivered one of several papers presented by both sides.[18]

In 1988 and 1993, he traveled to South Africa at the invitation of Archbishop Desmond Tutu, with whom he developed a warm friendship. On the first trip, Dyer addressed a conference of Anglican bishops, and on the second, he visited Nelson Mandela, who would become South Africa's first black head of state a year later with the collapse of the all-white government that Tutu and the Anglican Church had condemned so strongly.[19,20]

During his time as bishop, Dyer also developed a close friendship with the Rt. Rev. Walton Empey of the Diocese of Meath and Kildare in Ireland. They met in the run-up to the 1988 Lambeth Conference and bonded instantly. "It really happened so quickly," said Empey, who became Archbishop of Dublin in 1996 and retired in 2002. "I wasn't with him an hour before I realized that there was something very different about this man. I recognized it straightaway. There was depth, warmth, and humility. I can't say I was in awe of Mark. That would be wrong. He wasn't one to inspire awe. He was one to inspire the best that was in you."

As their friendship deepened, they developed plans for an exchange program between their dioceses. Dyer and Cluett returned to work with Empey's clergy, and there were youth visits. On one occasion, Dyer led a day of meditations at the cathedral in Kildare on the Gospels of Matthew, Mark, and Luke. The heat went off during the day but not one spellbound listener left early. "He made the scripture just leap out of the pages. That's the only way I can describe it. I would listen to [the tapes of Mark's talks] late at night when I was driving around the diocese and be refreshed all over again. I literally wore them out," Empey said.

Late in Dyer's tenure as bishop, Empey came to Bethlehem for three months with his wife to fill in for Dyer, who was recovering from hip replacement surgery. As he went around the diocese, "I realized why Mark was so much loved there," Empey said. "This was Mark, the warmth of the man, and the outreach of the man, and his ability to see what the needs were, and his ability to persuade people to carry out that vision because you can't do it on your own. Mark had that gift."

Empey, who became Archbishop of Dublin not long afterward, said that seeing the mission projects underway in Dyer's diocese "opened my eyes to all the ideas that we did not do in Ireland," something he set out to change after becoming archbishop.[21]

A Man on a Mission

This was way up in Appalachia. These were coal people. We had about nineteen people in church on Sunday. There was no way they could do anything, really, because they didn't have any money. So I went up there. In coal country, you could be Almighty God and they would still talk back to you. They are a tough bunch. . . . So I said, "You gotta find where the mission need is and I gotta find where the money is." My predecessor had made an attempt to close them down. I came there and said the bishop of this diocese doesn't shut anybody down. . . . They said, "You're crazy, Bishop. The other bishop wanted to throw us out and you want us to raise money for mission." I loved those coal people. They were so honest and so direct.[22] —Mark Dyer

"Mission is the lifeline of a parish or diocese,"[23] Dyer often said, and he began looking for ways to help his congregations put faith into action. He didn't have to look far—just down the hill, in fact—to get started.

A few hundred yards down Wyandotte Street from the cathedral in Bethlehem were three ramshackle buildings the diocese had bought for a song in 1979. It seems that the former owner was a gambling man who put up the buildings as collateral during a trip to Las Vegas where he lost everything. "So I got a call from a California bank," recalled Robert C. Wilkins, then the chief financial officer of Bethlehem Steel and the diocesan treasurer, "offering to sell us the properties at the debt value that the bank had absorbed. It was a bargain we couldn't turn down."[24]

It had taken several years for the tenants to move out, and the structures needed extensive and costly renovation. But where others saw obstacles, Dyer saw opportunity.

At one point, when he and Wilkins were trying to figure out how they could make things work financially, Dyer said, "Bob looked at me and said, 'You're crazy.' I said, 'No, Jesus is crazy and I'm following him.'"[25]

"Mark became bishop and inherited a mess in motion with no particular goal in mind," Wilkins said. "There was a group of five clergy from different denominations who were performing different mission programs including food, clothing, shelter, and counseling in separate locations. Mark proposed pulling it all together and housing them in the new building. Once this idea began to gel, someone suggested getting state grants and pulling it all together under one umbrella—which became the natural outgrowth of the seed Mark planted—and New Bethany Ministries [named by Dyer] was born."

The part of the complex used for temporary housing was a former rooming house. "It was pretty low-price and the clientele was not necessarily very reputable," Wilkins said with a wry smile. "And in the basement was a very active and popular restaurant."[26] When it opened in 1985 with twenty residents, the building was quickly dubbed by wags in the Episcopal ranks as "The Bishop's Bar and Brothel," a story Dyer delighted in recounting for the rest of his days.

More than thirty years later, New Bethany had grown into a healthy, self-sustaining nonprofit offering various transitional and temporary housing programs, a well-stocked food pantry, two hot meals a day for those in need, and job counseling. "Call it my field of dreams. I said, 'Build it and they will come,'" Dyer told *The Morning Call* newspaper in Allentown in his final interview before he retired as bishop. "That's what the business of the Christian church is all about—providing sanctuary, a safe place for broken and vulnerable people to come and feel they have a future."[27]

For Dyer, there was powerful symbolism in the location of this center of mission work next door to diocesan headquarters and within sight of the diocesan cathedral. And he made sure everyone knew it. "I always loved his parable about the way these buildings [were arranged]—the cathedral at one end with all of the beautiful vestments and finery and the diocesan house in the middle and New Bethany Ministries, where we serve the poor," said Social Missioner Allen. "And I will never forget him saying, 'It's only because of New Bethany that we are allowed to have these grand services at the cathedral. Only our ministry at New Bethany gives us the right to do that.' It was New Bethany that made us consistent with what he thought the gospel was calling us to be and do."

Dyer's insistence that every aspect of mission work, no matter how small or how large, had to be theologically grounded was new to Allen. "I wasn't used to a bishop being so concerned about making sure everything was theologically sound," Allen said. "That theological rigor and being able to articulate it—having the discipline to do that—was something I needed to learn how to do, and he taught me."

Allen added, "He was clear that our ministry with the poor and marginalized was a primary way that the Holy Spirit's work in the church was revealed to the world." Allen would help Dyer take his passion for mission from a street corner in downtown Bethlehem to every corner of the diocese.

In 1983, the Episcopal Church began issuing grants to help create Jubilee Centers in individual parishes to support local mission projects. Allen's first thought was to apply for these grants in some of the diocese's parishes. But then he and Dyer hatched a bigger and better idea, something no one else had done. "We said, 'Let's apply to be a Jubilee Diocese where we show that every congregation has a ministry of advocacy and outreach to the poor and the marginalized.' And everybody got caught up in that," Allen said. "I don't know any other diocese that was that bold. And that was very much in keeping with [Mark's beliefs]. We developed mission projects in places where no one thought they could have a mission project."[28]

Case in point: Tamaqua, Pennsylvania, a tiny, hardscrabble coal mining town where the coal had mostly played out, the economy was moribund, and Calvary Episcopal Church was struggling to keep its doors open. "The northern part of the Diocese of Bethlehem had no money, but those years were as rich as any I have ever had because the people were alive with the Holy Spirit," Dyer said. And they were willing to tackle mission work.

"They needed a senior day care center because we had the phenomenon of retired people still taking care of their parents," Dyer said. "So they renovated the parish hall, the local agency for aging came up with some money, and it's still there today with a consistent funding stream."[29]

From Tamaqua's senior center to "Every Child Is A Blessing," a national award-winning video featuring after-school and other social ministries in Pottsville, Wilkes-Barre, Allentown, and Bethlehem, mission projects spread like wildfire. Within three years, every parish in the diocese had one.

In 1994, the Diocese of Bethlehem was named the first—and so far the only—Jubilee Diocese in the Episcopal Church. In making the designation, which included a $25,000 grant, Episcopal Church representative Ntsiki Kabane-Langford said, "We are forming a partnership with this diocese to provide a dynamic model for the whole church. Your bishop will always be known as the bishop who left a legacy of social outreach ministry." Dyer replied, "Ntsiki touched my heart. If all I'm ever remembered for is as one who had a heart for the poorest of the poor, you will honor me greatly because I do know that to be the heart of Jesus Christ."[30]

But social outreach ministry also brought its own set of challenges for Dyer. "Mark was not pro-choice when I got here," Allen said. "He still had some of that Roman Catholic unease about abortion. And we were right in the thick of women's issues. The Jubilee Committee was a pretty diverse group and almost attracted to the hard issues and calling the church to say something about the hard issues. So they were kind of the fly in the ointment in a smooth-running diocese. But Mark appreciated the Jubilee Committee, and while they were a pain in the ass to him a lot of times, he never, ever said they should not be calling us to do the things they were calling us to do."[31]

Scandal

The phone call came at 10:00 on a Sunday night in early 1992. It was from the desk sergeant at the Bethlehem police department.

"They called me because they knew me," Dyer said. "The guy said, 'I have got some bad news for you. We usually don't tell someone in authority like you before we act, but you have someone over there who has been accused of hundreds of acts of pedophilia. We will be there at eleven in the morning and I just wanted to give you a head's up.' "

Within minutes Dyer summoned staff to his home. He knew instinctively that such a scandal could have a devastating impact on the diocese. Rather than devise a plan to stonewall the press and public and hope to ride out the storm, Dyer told his aides that he would do exactly the opposite. "I said, we are going have a press conference," Dyer recalled. "I want to be there when the police carry him away. I want this to be as public as possible. . . . I told them at the press conference, if you want more information and I can appropriately give it to you, just come into my office and you will get it. For me, it was just common sense."[32]

The extent of the criminal charges was staggering. Adam Tannous, the sixty-year-old sexton at St. Stephen's Episcopal Church in Whitehall Township, was charged with more than four thousand counts of sexually assaulting boys in the parish. To make matters worse, Tannous was a defrocked Episcopal priest who also volunteered as a youth group advisor at the church.[33]

In addition to his public statement, Dyer immediately sent a letter to the St. Stephen's congregation, reinforcing the theme of full disclosure. "Although I deeply regret the pain already felt and the scars around that wound," he wrote, "I am gratified that no attempt has been made to deny or to cover up the allegation that a serious tragedy has occurred. I encourage anyone who has been affected by this situation or who knows anything related to it to disclose fully to the appropriate authorities all relevant information."[34]

Dyer said Episcopal Church officials told him that church lawyers could handle everything for the diocese, but he said no. " 'Well,' I said, 'let's get one thing straight—this is my diocese and this is not your diocese. And you do what I tell you you can and can't do. Is that clear? So disappear, friends.' They were furious with me in New

York [at the Episcopal Church headquarters]. But I said we are simply not going to open up the diocese in that way."[35] Instead of being surrounded by a phalanx of lawyers, Dyer visited the victims and their families in their homes, and he sat with them in court.

Dyer's commitment to transparency—the diocesan newspaper published a front-page story about the scandal—and his public support for the victims of these sex crimes differed radically from the cover-up tactics used by some other religious organizations facing similar issues. Perhaps most notably, the Catholic Archdiocese of Boston's efforts to conceal the sexual misdeeds of many of its priests caused a major scandal unearthed by *The Boston Globe*. The paper won a Pulitzer Prize for its efforts in 2003 and the story led to the Oscar-winning movie *Spotlight*. Tannous pled guilty and was given the maximum sentence—thirty-five to seventy years in prison—where he died eight years later.[36]

At sentencing, the Rev. John Wagner, then a deacon at St. Stephen's, gave a victim impact statement. His son was one of the abuse victims. "For twenty minutes, maybe half an hour, I was face-to-face with the judge," Wagner said many years later. "I wanted to feel anger and rage, but what I felt was a tremendous sense of peace. I didn't understand it. It didn't feel right. When I turned around to go back to my seat at a bench near the back of the courtroom, I saw Mark Dyer on his knees in prayer. Then I understood—he had brought the holy into the secular through prayer."

Dyer's ministry to Wagner and his family continued after the trial. "Through that whole process, I could not have asked for a bishop or a friend stronger than Mark Dyer. I will never forget how he dealt with me and our family at one of the darkest times of my life. I was trying to carry all of that, to minister to my own family, and to let Mark minister to me," Wagner said.[37]

Dyer had more ministering to do when the trial was over. "We are standing outside saying goodbye and the judge's clerk comes out," Dyer said. "He said, 'Bishop, the judge wants to see you. He asked if you would come back to [his] chambers.'"

"I went back and he had his feet on the desk. He said, 'Thank God you were here, Bishop. I hope you understand my problem.' I said, 'What is your problem?' He said, 'I was in a Catholic seminary up to my deacon year. I just realized it wasn't my vocation . . . it is really hurting my conscience that I sent a priest to prison for life.'

"I said, 'The first thing you have to understand is that the Commonwealth of Pennsylvania doesn't have anywhere else to put this guy. You don't have any choice.' Then we talked about it some more, which seemed to help."[38]

Family Life

After their move to Bethlehem, the Dyer family settled into a two-story suburban house with a small garden and cornfields nearby. There were new schools for Jennifer and John and a new routine, but life still centered around Matthew on the living room couch. With Dyer on the road several days a week, Marie Elizabeth had to shoulder more of the family responsibilities, including taking care of Matthew, than she had when he was a rector. "I think she really held the family together, especially with Matthew. In the early days, almost every Sunday when Mark would visit a parish, Marie Elizabeth would come along, carrying Matthew," Lewellis said.[39]

But things were different, and the children felt it. The tight-knit community of Christ Church in Hamilton no longer surrounded and nurtured them. "We weren't next door to the parish anymore with the community all around, so the dynamics of life changed," said Jennifer. "We were out there growing up in suburbia next to the cornfields, and my parents had their work to do."[40]

Dyer pitched in with parental duties as best he could. That often meant driving Jennifer and John to school in the mornings or to sports and music activities after school. The threesome would make the rounds in the family van with the radio blaring Casey Kasem's "American Top 40" hits and the bishop schooling his children in rock 'n' roll trivia. They shared his passion for music, and Dyer made sure to take them to hear one of his favorite groups—Chicago— when it played in Allentown.

Jennifer's passion was gymnastics, which also required her to take ballet, and John sang in a boys' choir. But while Jennifer excelled at everything she did, John struggled with his schoolwork and was diagnosed with type 1 diabetes, which meant he would be insulin-dependent for the rest of his life. Friends suggested that John be tested for the cause of his learning problems, but Marie Elizabeth resisted. "It was very hard for her to accept that John was not a normal child," said her brother, Michael Hamlin.[41] These issues would weigh heavily on the Dyers in the years to come.

During her annual extended visits, Dorothy Hamlin, Marie Elizabeth's mother, assisted with the children. A widow, when the Dyers lived in Hamilton she had begun the practice of spending six months with Marie Elizabeth and her family in the United States and six months with Michael and his family in England. Mrs. Hamlin took her turn with domestic chores, washing clothes, sewing, crocheting, and caring for Matthew. Remembered by the children as a proper British lady and stoic disciplinarian, she also proved to be a zealous coupon clipper and collector of S&H Green Stamps, which, along with washing and reusing plastic bags, were regular features of life in the frugal Dyer household.

Marie Elizabeth, ordained since 1980, was looking for ways to pursue her ministry more actively while also serving as the bishop's wife and linchpin of their family. The priesthood had been open to women in the Episcopal Church for less than a decade, and she was the only priest married to a bishop, so there was no template for what to do and how to do it. That sometimes put her in the spotlight, a place she did not like to be. Her unique family demands made her situation that much more daunting.

Nevertheless, inaction was not in Marie Elizabeth's DNA, so she set about doing whatever she could, however she could. She began a quilt ministry for residents of New Bethany Ministries, enlisting people to make 6- by 6-inch cloth squares that others sewed together into 4- by 5-foot quilts. Over the years, about one thousand formerly homeless people left New Bethany with the gift of a quilt.[42]

Restless, energetic, and bristling with opinions, she would sweep through the diocesan offices, peppering her husband's staff with questions and ideas. It got to the point where if a staff member saw her coming through the parking lot, word would quickly spread: "Man your battle stations—here comes Marie Elizabeth."

But what she wanted most of all was to serve in a church, where she could pursue her passions for preaching, pastoral care, and serving the disadvantaged. She got her wish when she became the part-time assistant rector of The Church of the Mediator in Allentown. After a good start, things went downhill. She got along well with the veteran rector who hired her, but when he retired, his successor was much less experienced and soon found himself clashing with his outspoken assistant, who also happened to be his bishop's wife. It was a prescription for a meltdown.

"When it came to his family, Mark was totally blind. He had such love for them and it was not rational," Cluett recalled. "When Marie Elizabeth was the cause of upheaval and dissension, he jumped in as a husband, not as a bishop."[43] Rather than bringing in an outside mediator, Dyer tried to mediate things himself, which did not go well. After he stepped back from the fray, the situation was redeemed with the help of consultants from the Alban Institute, and Marie Elizabeth moved to another church. She became rector of St. Elizabeth's, a small parish in Allentown that always seemed to be on the edge of folding. It was a perfect match, and she would stay there for the rest of her life.

Marie Elizabeth immediately connected with the community, knocking on doors in the working-class neighborhood, inviting residents to church, and offering to baptize their children. Soon the baptism business was booming and there were new people in the pews with fresh energy. "She was an excellent parish priest, a much better rector than she was an assistant. She had a great pastoral ministry," said Cluett. "She was a caring, gentle leader. They respected her, liked her, and loved her, and she them."[44]

Women's Ordination

By the time Dyer became a bishop in 1982, the nation and the Episcopal Church were on the cusp of momentous change regarding the status of women. Marie Elizabeth was already an Episcopal priest, she had scores of counterparts across the country, and a New York congresswoman named Geraldine Ferraro was two years away from running for vice president of the United States. Despite major gains in opportunities for women in less than a decade, more decades of change and confrontation would follow in the nation, not to mention in the Anglican Communion, where the status of women continued to be a supercharged issue in some quarters.

The question of whether women should become deacons, priests, and bishops in the Episcopal Church began to boil over shortly before Dyer joined the church in 1971. A year earlier, the General Convention split over whether to permit the ordination of women. The proposal was approved by the laity but narrowly defeated by the clergy and so did not take effect.[45]

After the proposal failed again at the 1973 General Convention, some proponents of women's ordination decided to act. On July 29, 1974, two retired bishops and one resigned bishop ordained eleven women as priests in Philadelphia. The group became known as the Philadelphia 11, and the action, although heavily criticized by some, forced the hand of the Episcopal Church.[46] The 1976 General

Convention, after much debate, approved the ordination of women.[47] The Lambeth Conference of the worldwide Anglican Communion, of which the U.S. Episcopal Church is a part, followed suit in 1978.[48]

Despite his Roman Catholic upbringing, Dyer was fully on board. "I was sort of tagged the Anglo-Catholic for women priests in 1976," he recalled. "I said, 'It's very, very, very simple. Who in the history of the New Testament could kneel at the foot of the cross and look up at it and say, 'Don't you know that's my blood and my bread?' That was a woman."[49]

When Dyer arrived in his new diocese, he found only a handful of women priests. But as he expressed support and encouragement for the ordination of women, other women began to explore whether they were called to the priesthood. One of them was the Very Rev. Robyn Szoke-Coolidge, then a teacher, who met Dyer in 1984. "He took an active role with his nominees and postulants that I have not seen a lot of bishops do. He literally journeyed with me and I knew he was praying for me as I was praying for him," she said. "If you ask me what his favorite phrase was, it would have been, 'Robyn, are you saying your prayers every day?' For him, that was a very important part of your formation as a priest. You meet people all along the way of your pilgrimage, and he was one who really walked the Emmaus Road with you."

In those early days of women's ordination, Dyer sent most of his female postulants to Moravian Theological Seminary in Bethlehem, a Christian institution open to students of various denominations. "I think he didn't think that any of the eleven Episcopal seminaries were quite ready for women," said Szoke-Coolidge, who earned an MDiv from Moravian and an STM from General Theological Seminary.

Dyer also knew there was considerable opposition to the ordination of women among Episcopalians in his diocese, and he set out to change hearts, minds, and habits. His approach, Szoke-Coolidge said, was "teaching, teaching, teaching," much as he did when he supported the celebration of the Holy Eucharist on every Sunday rather than monthly, in keeping with the 1979 Book of Common Prayer. She remembers meetings where clergy and laypeople, male and female, would gather in small groups, share their spiritual stories, and anoint each other with oil. The effect, she said, was powerful. "That's how he broke down barriers. Name the pain; accept the pain," said Szoke-Coolidge, who went on to become dean of the Stevenson School for Ministry of the Diocese of Central Pennsylvania.[50]

Human Sexuality

Issues of human sexuality emerged during this time as well, demanding attention and challenging long-held views and traditions. When New York City police raided the Stonewall Inn, a popular gay nightclub in Greenwich Village, on the night of June 28, 1969, it touched off six days of violent protests and marked a turning point in the gay rights movement in the United States and around the world. Once again, the church found itself in the middle of it all.

In the late 1960s, homosexuality was still considered a mental disorder by the American Psychiatric Association. Mainstream religions, including the Episcopal Church, had generally condemned homosexual behavior in the past, and gay sex was against the law in many places. As a result, the gay lifestyle had existed largely in the shadows. But gay men and women began coming forward, asserting their rights, and seeking acceptance and inclusion in society, including in the church.

Then came AIDS.

Dyer came to the Diocese of Bethlehem just two months after the U.S. Centers for Disease Control and Prevention began using the name "acquired immune deficiency syndrome," or AIDS, for the mysterious disease that was starting to kill Americans at an alarming rate. Later known as HIV/AIDS, the disease was on its way to becoming a worldwide epidemic, and scientists would discover that it was spread by unprotected sex. Infection rates among gay men were especially high.

By the time Scott Allen arrived as Social Missioner, the diocese was in a full-blown HIV/AIDS crisis. People were sick, people were dying, people were afraid. Though far out of his comfort zone in confronting the social issues enveloping the crisis, Dyer relied on his faith and his compassion.

Drawing on his experience in ministering to the sick and suffering with Mother Teresa's Missionaries of Charity, he plunged into this new ministry, reaching out personally to people and meeting them in their pain, fear, and suffering. He told his local newspaper, *The Morning Call*, "If you look into the eyes of someone with AIDS, you can see the face of God."[51]

"I admired Mark for his openness and willingness to listen, reflect, and hold off on pronouncements in favor of fostering a conversation among the community of the baptized to try to come to some consensus that was just and consistent with the gospel and tradition of the church," Allen said. A turning point for Dyer, said Allen, came when the Episcopal Church asked every member of the House of Bishops to develop a personal relationship with someone who had HIV/AIDS. "Mark intentionally came into a pastoral relationship with a person living with HIV/AIDS," Allen recalled. "David Houseknecht was a flamboyant, very public, and vocal person. This was a courageous move on Mark's part, as this was the era when many people were afraid of contagion at the altar rail and drinking from the common cup, and yes, even exchanging the peace with those with HIV/AIDS."[52]

On another occasion, Dyer was told that a young man dying of AIDS at home wanted to be received into the Episcopal Church. Arriving at the house, he found the man on the couch surrounded by family members and a hospice worker. "I went over and sat next to him, and we had a conversation about Christ," Dyer recalled.

"He said, 'Father, if I become an Episcopalian, do I have to give up Mary?' I said 'No, you don't.' I had my rosary in my pocket, and I took it out and put it in his hand. Then we said the prayers for the dying together."[53]

In November 1991, Dyer conducted a healing service at the cathedral in Bethlehem for people with HIV/AIDS and for those seeking ways to support them. Dyer laid hands on all—"modeling that these folks were not untouchables," said Allen[54]—while other clergy anointed the sick. At a news conference before the service, Dyer was asked if the AIDS virus was a punishment from God. "That would mean that God is sitting in heaven saying there are millions of people in the world that He doesn't like and He is going to make them die a long, slow, painful death. If one believes that, one is forced to believe God is a maniac," Dyer said.[55]

As Allen worked with Dyer to create an HIV/AIDS ministry, he sensed a change in his bishop. "I think HIV/AIDS made Mark more sympathetic to LGBT issues," he said. "Initially, at least in my estimation, Mark was not on the front row for inclusion of LGBT people, particularly in ordained ministry. He wasn't hateful, and he wasn't anti-LGBT in a mean way, but with Mark, everything had to be theological, everything had to do with reason, tradition, and scripture. And tradition and scripture did not make a lot of room for LGBT people. But I think he grew in that regard.

"All of that is to say that I respected Mark because he could change his mind. And he didn't just change his mind from pressure. It was a theological analysis and a really prayerful seeking that resulted in that change of mind." More than a decade later, when Allen revealed to Dyer that he was gay, he said Dyer was very supportive. "The first thing he said was, 'You know, Scott, this is not going to change our friendship in any way,'" Allen recalled. "By that point, I think he had softened a lot on that."[56]

Clearly, Dyer's views on human sexuality did evolve over a period of years, sometimes spilling into view as he wrestled with his thoughts. "I remember having a conversation with him about human sexuality at one point and it was so convoluted that I really couldn't understand what he was saying to me,"[57] recalled the Most Rev. Frank T. Griswold, who was presiding bishop when the Episcopal Church consecrated its first openly gay bishop. Dyer's continuing journey of discovery on these issues would play out as part of the unfolding crisis that rocked the Episcopal Church and the Anglican Communion more than a decade later.

An Activist Bishop

Soft-spoken, reserved, and even somewhat shy, Dyer nonetheless developed a strong public persona within his own diocese and the church at large. A prolific writer who preferred pen, pencil, and paper to the computer that sat untouched on his desk, he churned out an array of sermons, pastoral letters, and columns and articles for newspapers and magazines, often collaborating with Lewellis.

Much of this writing was aimed at the grassroots level, but Dyer also produced more scholarly pieces on theology for the Episcopal Church's House of Bishops and for the Anglican Communion. And he issued ringing statements on the sometimes-heated issues of the day, of which there were many. While some Episcopal bishops in larger dioceses were grabbing headlines and defying church policy on such hot button issues as the ordination of women, same-sex marriage, and the ordination of homosexuals, Dyer spoke out forcefully—not squarely in opposition to such changes, but arguing instead for following church procedures and striving to build consensus in deciding these matters.

When the Diocese of Washington, DC, ordained a practicing homosexual to the priesthood in June 1991,[58] Dyer denounced the move. "I consider the recent unilateral action in the Diocese of Washington theologically irresponsible and a serious obstacle to our communion as Anglicans as well as to our relationships with other religious faiths and traditions," he said in a written statement. To him, the issue was one of process, not morality.

The Episcopal Church had decided in 1979 that practicing homosexuals or people engaged in sexual relationships outside of marriage should not be ordained, and that policy was still in effect. The church's General Convention was scheduled to convene one month after the ordination in the Diocese of Washington, and Dyer argued that any such action by a diocese was totally inappropriate until the issue was properly settled by the church's governing authority. "The issue of the ordination of practicing homosexuals can be addressed neither appropriately nor responsibly until the Church comes to a common understanding of human sexuality," he said.[59]

When Congress authorized President George H.W. Bush to commence hostilities in the Persian Gulf War, Dyer opposed the move, cataloguing the evils of war and citing his own service in the Korean War. But he also said, "I will pray from this moment on that I am wrong and that the forty-nine senators who voted against going to war are wrong."[60]

In an era before "branding" leapt from the business school lexicon to the general vocabulary, Dyer was building his own brand as a mainstream spiritual leader who applied traditional principles of faith and the teachings of Jesus to find theologically sound ways to address contentious contemporary issues. His unique blend of Catholic and Protestant spirituality, along with his compelling personal story of a Korean War veteran who became a Benedictine monk and then an Episcopal priest and bishop, made him a distinct and engaging figure who might have stepped out of central casting to play a leading role in a modern morality play.

Episcopalians in the Diocese of Bethlehem were used to an activist bishop. Gressle had marched with Father Daniel Berrigan to protest the Vietnam War and had urged Governor Milton Shapp to veto legislation that would have eliminated abortions in Pennsylvania. They watched Dyer with a growing sense of interest and pride. He was not afraid to tell his version of truth to power and challenge the reigning assumptions of the day.

He led the diocese in condemning legalized gambling and endorsing progressive positions on protecting the environment. The Diocesan Council voted in 1984 to oppose casinos, slot machines, "and all attempts by state and local governments to raise revenues through gambling as an alternative to taxation," with Dyer calling the practice "demonic" and noting that "the losers are those who are already at the bottom of the social and economic ladder."[61]

Dyer created a task force in 1990 to champion environmental education and advocacy. In doing so, he linked environmental stewardship with religious responsibilities and values: "To deface creation is to deface the very character of God's revelation. That's how serious the issue of the environment is. It has a lot to do with the economy. It has a lot to do with the air we breathe. But theologically, it has everything to do with the revelation of God. This is the basic theological reality all religions share."[62]

Increasingly, his voice was heard nationally throughout the Episcopal Church and internationally throughout the Anglican Communion as he became a trusted advisor and confidant to three successive Archbishops of Canterbury and undertook sensitive missions on their behalf. His Anglican Communion work meant more and more time away from his diocese, but the Episcopalians of northeastern Pennsylvania did not seem to mind. "He traveled the world and they were proud of him. They did not feel neglected," said the Rt. Rev. Sean Rowe, bishop of the Diocese of Northwestern Pennsylvania, who also became provisional bishop of the Diocese of Bethlehem in 2014 after Dyer's successor stepped down. "He was gone a substantial amount of time . . . but in no way did they feel that they had been abandoned or that his ambitions were greater than they were."[63]

As Dyer's tenure entered a new decade, his prominence grew. There were honorary degrees from the Episcopal Seminary of the

Southwest and from Muhlenberg College, and possibilities for other ministries presented themselves. In 1990, when he was under consideration to become an archbishop of the Anglican Church of Australia, he and Marie Elizabeth flew to Melbourne to get a sense of what ministry there would be like. Though honored at being considered, Dyer quickly concluded that the job was too rich for his blood. "It just never fit me," he said years later. "Everywhere I went would be in a chauffeured car with a flag on the front. I just said 'I simply don't want this kind of life. I am a priest.' "[64]

There were also feelers about his becoming bishop of the Convocation of Episcopal Churches in Europe, joining the School of Theology at the University of the South in Sewanee, Tennessee, or teaching at General Theological Seminary in New York. Notwithstanding these possibilities, Dyer remained in Bethlehem, but there was a definite sense of winding down. "There came a time he felt he had done what he could here," Cluett said. "He hoped to return to teaching and the academic community."[65]

That opportunity would come, though not in the form he first thought it would.

Benedictine Bedrock

Dyer left a substantial legacy among the laypeople and clergy of the Diocese of Bethlehem in the form of his deep spirituality, his passion for mission work, his devotion to pastoral care, and in the love, joy, and faith he so freely shared. His was a ministry of service and teaching built on Benedictine theological bedrock. "As bishops go, we don't have a lot of that combination—at least I haven't seen it—of being theologically sharp, scripturally sound, and totally mission-oriented. For Mark, it was all about bringing the gospel to the world," Allen said.[66]

"His legacy has continued largely. Congregations are pretty socially aware. They are keeping the doors open and serving the community," said Rowe. "Those small places especially remember him. They talk about him coming and offering words of encouragement at times when they thought they would likely close. He offered them spiritual guidance to persevere, to seek God. When Mark came, this is what they heard. They would want what he wanted because it seemed right. He could make you want what he wanted.

"Mark did not deliver at the granular level. He delivered at the visionary level," Rowe continued. "He didn't want much to do with the finances or the canons. He was a teacher. He studied the Bible regularly with the clergy."[67]

"There was a real devotion to him in a certain circle of folks," said church communications consultant Jim Naughton. "It really does feel like it was the high point of their lives. It's quite something, really."[68]

Bob Wilkins forged a strong bond with Dyer. They were the same age and served in the same navy task force during the Korean War. Wilkins will never forget Dyer's pastoral side. "My wife had a heart attack," Wilkins said. "She was at St. Luke's, and the doctors were talking like she didn't have long to go. I asked Mark to say a prayer for her. But he didn't just do that. He got in his car and drove to the hospital. When I walked into the room, he had Kathy's head in his hands and he was in her face, in her soul, I think. She had been basically in a coma, but she came out of it while he held her in his hands. And she never had a problem since. I think she is here because of him."

Wilkins also marveled at Dyer's ability to connect with people from all walks of life. "You could sit and talk to the man. He was an intellectual, he was known internationally, he was many, many things to many people, but he could sit down with the most ordinary people in the world and make you feel like there was nothing more important than what you had to say," Wilkins recalled.[69]

The Rev. Canon Gwendolyn-Jane Romeril also noted Dyer's exceptional gift for relating to people and thought she knew how he was able to do that. As Dyer prepared to retire as bishop in late 1995, she wrote, "I remember when Mark told me that he always tries to imagine a veil between himself and another person, and imprinted on that veil is the face of Christ."[70]

Upon his departure for Virginia Theological Seminary, the diocese presented Dyer and Marie Elizabeth with a painstakingly assembled scrapbook brimming with remembrances and handwritten thank-you notes from clergy, vestry members, confirmands, HIV/AIDS activists, Sunday school students and teachers, and all manner of laypeople from across the diocese. Perhaps this line from a letter from Trinity Church in Bethlehem best summed up the feelings of Dyer's flock about their bishop: "You have lifted this diocese and each parish to a new level of spirituality and awareness of God and God's mission to the world."

CHAPTER 9

A Yankee in the Archbishop of Canterbury's Court

As my wife, Marie Elizabeth was the only woman priest at the Lambeth Conference in 1988. I was on the steering committee of the conference and, as usual, the queen had a dinner for us. We had an opportunity to meet the whole royal family, so my wife went to Edmond Browning, the presiding bishop, and she said, "Ed, what do we do?" And he said, "You should go."

So we lined up. The queen was very polite and is a lovely lady who has a wonderful gift of service and hospitality. . . . Princess Diana talked with us for a long time. Then Prince Philip comes over and he says to me, "You've got a purple shirt on." Well, if there was such a thing as being an expert in insulting people, then he's an expert. And then he says, talking about Marie Elizabeth, "But you're a bishop and she's a priest in the same diocese." I said yes, and he said, "That's wrong. If the time comes that she becomes a parish priest, then you would be appointing her. And I don't think you should be doing that." So I said, "Well, the royalty knows more about putting people in jobs who shouldn't be there."

And he got mad at me, and Marie Elizabeth kicked me on the ankle. But I wasn't going to let him get away with that. An Englishman doesn't charge an Irishman.[1]
—Mark Dyer

So just how, exactly, did a former Benedictine monk from a blue-collar neighborhood in Manchester, New Hampshire, come to be a confidant and trusted advisor to three archbishops of Canterbury, travel the world on behalf of the Anglican Communion, lead complex and sensitive theological discussions with the Eastern Orthodox Church, and help craft some of the most respected theological statements for the Communion in the late twentieth century?

The answer is rooted in Dyer's deep wells of spiritual insight that produced a gentle, monastic gravitas and in a network of trusting personal relationships he developed with influential religious leaders. His close bond with Robin Eames, for example, an Irish bishop when they first met who later became Archbishop of Armagh and Primate of All Ireland, gave him access to the highest level of the Anglican Communion hierarchy. "Mark was warm, down to earth, always open, and we had trust and confidence in each other," Eames said. "So it was just that we welcomed Mark, we trusted Mark, and I think Mark trusted us. . . . I think it was just on a basis of friendship, but he certainly was, for most of us, the acceptable face of the Episcopal Church."[2]

Dyer had found his spiritual home in Anglicanism. Now fully in his element, he delighted in its liturgies and embraced its traditions, assigning a special place in his heart for Thomas Cranmer's Book of Common Prayer. "Cranmer knew the medieval church and his

dream was in the title—The Book of Common Prayer. He was saying, 'Now here are your tools,'" Dyer said.[3]

Given his deep commitment to ecumenical and interfaith relations, he was also at the right place at the right time. Robert Runcie,
who became Archbishop of Canterbury in 1980, convened an historic
meeting in London with Pope John Paul II in 1982—the same year
Dyer became a bishop—to explore possibilities for reuniting those
branches of Christianity. Also, a dialogue between the Anglican
Communion and the Eastern Orthodox Church, begun in 1973, finished its second phase in 1984 but had gone dormant and was in need
of a restart.

In the United States, Dyer's friend Edmond Lee Browning
became presiding bishop of the Episcopal Church in 1986. Dyer
had led spiritual retreats in Browning's home diocese of Hawaii, and
Browning knew of Dyer's devotion to the Anglican Communion and
interfaith dialogue.

Within two years, Browning recommended to Runcie that Dyer
be appointed as the only American on an eight-member committee of
international Anglican representatives charged with preserving harmony in the Communion after a contentious Lambeth Conference in
1988 that cleared the way for women to become bishops but allowed
regional autonomy in deciding whether to permit it.

When Dyer's appointment was announced, Browning said he
had chosen him "because I know that he will bring to that role both
his considerable theological insights and his understanding of the
gifts of ordained women."[4] (Browning and Dyer were both already
on record as supporting the consecration of women bishops.)

Dyer served on the Steering Committee for the Lambeth
Conference of 1988, and in that role was one of twenty bishops (and
the only American) from around the world who prepared theological
position papers and the conference agenda. First convened by the
Archbishop of Canterbury in 1867 and continuing every ten years in

England with only occasional interruptions, Lambeth Conferences bring together Anglican bishops from throughout the Communion to discuss and consult on issues of the day. Though not a governing authority, the conferences' deliberations and resolutions are highly influential within the Communion.

Dyer had come to Runcie's attention thanks to Eames, who had been dispatched to the United States by Runcie in the 1980s on a diplomatic and intelligence-gathering mission to sound out American Episcopal leaders on their feelings about their relationship with the Anglican Communion and what the future might hold. Eames connected with Dyer as he made his rounds, and the two established an instant rapport.

"Mark introduced himself to me with 'I have Irish roots, Robin,'" Eames recalled. "'Oh, I said, have you? What were those?' And he started into his diatribe about Sligo and his ancestry back there. . . . We warmed to each other . . . so that when we started to talk about serious matters, there was already the basis of a man-to-man friendship and we were at ease with each other."[5] Grounded in this personal relationship, the two genial Irishmen forged a working partnership that would last more than fifteen years and provide opportunities for them to shape theological statements addressing a series of divisive global issues that would shake the very foundations of the Anglican Communion.

That partnership began as Eames strove to grasp the American Episcopal Church's state of mind about its relationship with the Anglican Communion, headquartered in England. The two nations were longtime allies, but sentiments on some issues as old as the American Revolution still ran deep. "There was a feeling among some, particularly on your side of the pond, that Canterbury might exert too much of a 'This is the way you do it,' colonial sort of approach. [The Americans] wanted to be part of [the Anglican Communion] but they also wanted to maintain their independence," Eames recalled years later.

"The contribution Mark made first for the relations between the two churches was that he wanted an easygoing understanding, and out of that developed the whole idea," Eames said. With Dyer's input, Eames devised "a suggested formula whereby the Episcopal Church would have its own setup—independent—but would adhere to the principles of the Anglican Communion and allow for bonds of affection between the two."

But that wasn't all. During Eames's trip to America, he and Dyer also engaged in discussions that often ran deep into the night about the Anglican Communion's relationship with the Eastern Orthodox Church and the prospect of another round of ground-breaking dialogue. "We never dreamt that might be possible—encourage it," Runcie told Eames, who extended his stay in the United States to nail down more details.

"We had started to examine the relationship between the Episcopal Church and Canterbury," Eames said, "but we ended up developing a new relationship with the Orthodox. And Mark Dyer, I would say, was 90 percent responsible for that."[6]

Runcie, a decisive sort who was a decorated World War II tank unit commander, took Dyer's measure in the preparations for the 1988 Lambeth Conference and at the conference itself. He liked what he saw, and Dyer's standing grew accordingly. After appointing Dyer as chairman of the theology section for the conference, Runcie told him, "Don't worry—I've got two young scholars to help you out."[7] Dyer's helpers, Rowan Williams and Stephen Sykes, were to become leading theologians and bishops; Williams became Archbishop of Canterbury (2002–2012). "I can imagine that Mark's presence and perspective would have been something that Robert Runcie would have warmed to, and Robert was a great talent spotter," said Williams.[8]

At lunch on the last day of the conference, Runcie stopped by Dyer's table and placed a sealed envelope by his plate.

"Thank you, Your Grace," Dyer said. "I'll read it on the plane and respond as soon as I get home."

"You don't have to answer," Runcie replied. "I've got a job for you. That's how it works."

"Yes, Your Grace," said Dyer, offering the safest answer he could think of.

"It's an old job of mine and I want you to do it," Runcie said. End of discussion.[9]

The Orthodox Theological Dialogues

> So I went to my first meeting with the leaders of the Eastern Orthodox Church. They were from all of the ancient sees and they introduced themselves—"I am the metropolitan from Alexandria, and I am the bishop from Antioch, and I am the metropolitan from Cyprus," and so on. They really poured it on. Byzantine was an adjective with these guys. Then it was my turn and I said, "I am very impressed but don't you realize that it all started with me? I'm the bishop of Bethlehem!"[10] —Mark Dyer

It was September 1990, and Mark Dyer was in Toronto leading a team of Anglican clergy who were meeting with a team of Eastern Orthodox prelates from some of the most famous and ancient sees in Christendom to begin a new round of theological dialogue. He was the new kid on the block, but his opening gambit had disarmed his Orthodox counterparts.

Rowan Williams, who at the time was a rapidly rising clergyman, scholar, and a member of the Anglican delegation, thought it was a perfect icebreaker. "It allowed him to locate himself on their map a bit. But even more," Williams said, "I think it was that hinterland of his monastic formation that put him on the map that they recognized."[11]

This was the third round of dialogue since 1973 between these two branches of Christianity that had a considerable global presence—the Orthodox with more than 200 million members and the Anglicans with 70 million. The two earlier rounds had produced two statements of agreement after meetings in Dublin and Moscow, but the process had since ground to a halt.

"The Dublin and Moscow statements had laid the foundations, but women's ordination derailed the dialogues," said the Rt. Rev. Gregory Cameron, who became co-secretary of the Anglican-Orthodox dialogue in 2003. "The Orthodox had stopped the dialogues. Mark was the person entrusted [with] getting the dialogues going again."[12]

Why did Runcie think Dyer would be a good fit for the job?

Williams offered this perspective: "He was the perfect Anglican presence . . . I think, because he represented for the Orthodox something they could take seriously. Mark evidently was somebody they understood, somebody who, with his theological and spiritual interiority, had a real credibility for them.

"He wasn't somebody who was formed by or shaped by a particular internal Anglican agenda. He had a concern for that wholeness of the tradition, which was very significant in that context, oddly enough representing the Anglican world to the Orthodox world as somebody who wasn't a cradle Anglican. But it worked."[13]

The Rev. Dr. James Farwell, a colleague of Dyer's years later at Virginia Theological Seminary, said Dyer was effective in the dialogues because "he was both a charmer and a warrior. The Orthodox are lovely and brilliant and rooted into a tradition that Westerners don't tap into as we should, but they also can be a very prickly bunch. I think it was that story-telling, merry, raconteur thing that Mark could be that enabled him to disarm some of the prickliness of his Orthodox interlocutors while at the same time be a warrior for this Anglican vision as it had developed for him."[14]

. Rev. David Hamid, who was co-secretary of the Anglican-Or... dialogue from 1998–2002, observed another reason for Dyer's bond with the Orthodox. "One thing that I think really endeared him to the Orthodox was that he was a theologian, pastor, and bishop, but he also never wanted to divorce theology from spirituality, which was very dear to them. That's the Orthodox part—that you only really do theology as you are praying. That was Mark as well, so that made him a very congenial dialogue partner for them," Hamid said.[15]

The Rev. Canon John Gibaut, who joined the talks in 1994 as a representative of the Anglican Church of Canada, agreed. "The Orthodox had tremendous respect for Mark and his integrity," he said. "For the Orthodox, personal holiness counts the way doctoral degrees would count for Anglicans. And I think that was part of what made Mark such a successful co-chair."[16]

Dyer's Eastern Orthodox counterpart as co-chair of the International Commission for Anglican-Orthodox Theological Dialogue was Metropolitan John Zizioulas of Pergamon, one of the leading Orthodox theologians in the world. In many ways, Zizioulas and Dyer were polar opposites. Brilliant, opinionated, and acerbic at times, Zizioulas did not suffer fools lightly and sometimes expressed witheringly critical comments during theological discussions. If anything, he was harder on the Orthodox participants than he was on the Anglicans.

But he and Dyer developed a remarkable relationship that allowed not only for free-flowing debate but also for each to use his gifts to greatest effect—Zizioulas as an instigator of profound theological dialogue, which Dyer loved and engaged in to the fullest, and Dyer as more of a pastoral, inclusive consensus-builder. "You've got John Zizioulas, who is this brilliant speculative thinker, and you've got Mark Dyer, who is a brilliant strategist and an ecclesiological theologian who knows the tradition and wants to ground things in that tradition" said Gibaut. "The two of them were equally brilliant in different ways, complementary ways. They were a fantastic team."[17]

Dyer's role changed somewhat when Williams left the dialogue in 2002 to take up his duties as Archbishop of Canterbury. "Rowan had been a great sparring partner of John Zizioulas," Cameron said. "It fell to Mark to take over the role, and he became, really, the chief patristic scholar on the commission. Mark could carry the battle into the patristic field and quote from the patristic texts.

"The relationship between John and Mark was warm and respectful," Cameron added. "Tensions were not between co-chairs; they nearly always were between their teams." As co-chairs, Zizioulas and Dyer enjoyed occasionally lobbing a rhetorical grenade into a theological discussion "to really get it going," Cameron recalled.[18]

"It was like having a constant post-graduate seminar in theology going on all the time," said Hamid. "There were times in that dialogue when the rest of the commission would just sit back and let John and Mark go at it. I remember so many occasions when literally around the table we just felt like, 'Well, let's let the two experts hammer this out and see where the chips fall.' But it was always really very affectionate—both the ecumenical work and the theological work. There was a real community among the people around the table. We felt we were working on a very important agenda but working at it together."

Hamid credited Dyer for nurturing that sense of community among the dialogue members. "He was a very gentle and patient chair, and that helped to keep things moving. People really felt like they were being respected and listened to. He was very forgiving and he was never going to embarrass you because you had ventured a thought that was a bit wrong," Hamid said.[19]

Cameron agreed. "Mark had a sense of where he wanted to go, but he didn't crack the whip over the delegation. He governed by gentility," he said.

Yet each co-chairman had his pet peeves. "John could get frustrated with Orthodox theologians' inability to see the other side of an argument," Cameron said. "Mark got frustrated with Anglicans that didn't come up with the goods. Working members had to write a good paper with references."[20] But where Zizioulas would erupt publicly, Dyer would address his issues privately.

Even when things were going well, however, the very nature of theological dialogue meant that there were times of exhaustive, seemingly endless discussion and parsing of translations of scripture that could tax the patience of even the most patient participants. "Dialogue is a very wonderful thing but it certainly grinds the teeth at times," said Williams, adding that he and Dyer shared moments of exasperation with the process. "But the sense always was that here was a profoundly understanding moderator [Dyer] of the discussion who would, even within that context, be drawing the best out of people."[21]

Yet there were times that Dyer had to lead forcefully, especially among the Anglicans. "The Anglicans, in any other context, would have been at each other's throats about any number of things," said Gibaut. "But we [weren't], and I think that, in part, was the steadying influence of Mark, who was able to put brakes on things when things needed braking."

Gibaut remembered one meeting at Canterbury when an Anglican bishop wanted to raise the issue of human sexuality even though Zizioulas had said the topic would not be discussed at that time. Meeting with the Anglican caucus beforehand, Dyer confronted the issue head-on. "He said, 'Look, we're not going there, everybody. We're just not going there. This is not on this agenda.' And we didn't go there," Gibaut said.

Presiding at dialogue meetings when both sides were present called for as much diplomacy as leadership. "Mark just shone in the diplomacy," Gibaut said. "He could say all the right things; he could say very difficult things but in ways that were firm and clear and not hurtful." What's more, Dyer infused his Anglican colleagues with his values of teamwork, respect, and collegiality, so the team functioned as if he were there even when he wasn't, "which was a remarkable thing," Gibaut said.[22]

The talks lasted for seventeen years, convening informally and formally in exotic, historic locales such as Addis Ababa, Bucharest, Istanbul, and concluding in Cyprus in 2005. Much of the sensitive work was done in informal meetings, when no minutes were kept. "That's where developments around, say, the ordination of women, would be raised for response personally rather than reading about it in the paper," Gibaut said. "But a lot of it was just sheer diplomacy with a lot of eating and a lot of praying."

Through it all, Dyer and Zizioulas managed to steer the dialogue around treacherous theological shoals, inching forward on a number of fronts. The challenge in creating such documents, Gibaut said, is "Not just what we can agree to say together, but what we can agree to say together that takes the project a little bit further. . . . What can we say together that moves both of our churches slightly beyond where we were? That was tricky writing, but it was Mark who got me to do that."[23]

What emerged from these talks in 2006 was a document, known as The Cyprus Statement and titled *The Church of the Triune God*. Remarkable in scope, it somehow managed to open the door to a continuing theological conversation about one of the most divisive issues of the day—the ordination of women—rather than slamming it shut.

"Mark never explicitly said in that dialogue that you must logically accept the possibility of women being ordained on these theological principles," Hamid recalled. "But people knew that everything he was arguing theologically meant that one therefore had to accept the ordination of women. And the Orthodox knew this as well. . . . It was a remarkable thing for the Orthodox to have signed onto."[24]

Cameron called the statement "a landmark achievement" in Anglican-Orthodox dialogue. "Mark and John began with the patristic style, asking 'What do we believe about God? What we believe about God tells us what we believe about the church. And if this is what we believe about the church, then what do we believe about the priesthood, and can women partake of the priesthood?'" he said.[25] While the report recognized that the Anglican and Orthodox churches did not agree that women should be ordained as priests, the Orthodox expressed appreciation "for the pastoral motivation that has led the Anglican Communion to ordain women," and the statement concluded that "the theological dimension of this matter remains open and deserves further and deeper consideration and study in ecumenical dialogue."[26]

"Through their very good double act, John and Mark got us to the theological position that [the ordination of women] was an open theological question," Cameron said. "There was no way to get the Orthodox to agree to ordain women, but an open theological question means that it has not been defined as heretical, so it opened the way to a third phase of theological dialogue."[27]

Yet while *The Church of the Triune God* continues to draw praise from key quarters for its theology and scholarship, it has had little lasting impact. "I consider *The Church of the Triune God* to be one of the most important texts of this phase of the ecumenical movement," said Gibaut. "It never got the hearing it ought to have because the 2008 Lambeth Conference was of a different format. It was designed to get the bishops to talk to each other rather than make decisions. And Lambeth Conferences are the place where a report like that would be received, discussed, argued, and commended to the churches. And that never happened. So it's a text still waiting to be properly received.

"It's still getting a reception from the academic community. It has hugely influenced a lot of people. And anyone who has reviewed that text thinks that it is just so far ahead of its time," he concluded.[28]

Dr. Timothy F. Sedgwick, a Virginia Theological Seminary professor who has closely followed Anglican affairs, agreed, calling the document "one of the best pieces of work on the nature of the church and the Anglican Communion. It advances and furthers and deepens our understanding of authority and the nature of communion and unity of the church."[29]

Rowan Williams said, "I think that statement is a really, really significant achievement and [Mark] has to take the bulk of the credit for that, because even though he was only half of the presidency, in practice he did all the heavy lifting and organization. . . . And what emerged, I think, was really a very, very solid piece of theological reflection, which, appropriately, will feed into the Communion's life in the long term.

"So bringing that to such a harmonious and fruitful conclusion will be, I think, one of his greatest legacies to the Communion, surely. And the fact that the dialogue went on demonstrates the seriousness with which that work was taken. . . . And, of course, it happened in spite of all the ups and downs in the Communion, which means that all the foundations were driven well down."[30]

The Church of the Triune God was formally presented to Williams and Bartholomew I, the Ecumenical Patriarch of the Eastern Orthodox Church, at a ceremony at Lambeth Palace in London on January 30, 2007. In an ironic historical footnote, the report had not come back from the printer at the time of the presentation, so the ceremonial document presented that day was actually a copy of the Windsor Report, vintage 2004. It was a closely guarded secret.

Williams recognized Dyer's contributions to the Anglican Communion by awarding him the Lambeth Cross, an honor reserved for those who have done exceptional work on behalf of relations between faiths. Williams had wanted to give Dyer an honorary Lambeth degree, but that would have required him to swear an oath of allegiance to Queen Elizabeth II, which Williams knew his friend, an American citizen and one with deep Irish roots at that, could never do.

CHAPTER 10

Of Women Priests
and Bishops

All Anglicans possess a common faith and a life of common prayer. From a confession of common faith follows a life of common prayer. One of the realities of the Anglican Communion is that we pray what we believe. Baptism and Eucharist are the entry into the identity of an Anglican all through the world.[1] —Mark Dyer

While Dyer was heavily engaged in the Anglican-Orthodox dialogues throughout the 1990s and still tending to the Diocese of Bethlehem, he served with Robin Eames on two commissions charged with the difficult task of helping the Anglican Communion find its way in addressing the issue of women serving as priests and bishops.

The triggering event was the 1988 Lambeth Conference, which witnessed two watershed events in the history of the Anglican Communion. First, the Episcopal Church stoked the fires of change by presenting a proposal to consecrate the first woman bishop in the

Communion when some parts of the Communion were still resisting the notion of women priests, much less bishops.

Second, 1988 marked a distinct power shift among Anglican bishops, as those representing parts of the world outside of traditional Anglican bastions in Europe and North America began to establish a numerical majority. Many in the new majority, including a number from African dioceses, held more conservative positions on scripture and social issues, opposed the ordination of women, and began to speak out more forcefully on such issues.[2]

When the 1988 Lambeth Conference concluded, it had cleared the way for women to become priests and bishops in the Anglican Church. In true Anglican fashion, the conference's action allowed women to be ordained, but did not specify how that would happen.

In the untidy aftermath of those decisions and non-decisions, Archbishop of Canterbury Robert Runcie named a commission in September 1988, chaired by Eames, to help sort things out. Officially called the Commission on Communion and Women in the Episcopate, it became known as the Eames Commission. The commission met five times and produced four reports, which were published together in December 1994. By that time, five women had been consecrated as Anglican bishops and more than one thousand women throughout the world had been ordained as Anglican priests. Parts of the Communion, especially the United States and Canada, moved quickly to embrace this change, while other parts of the Communion were strongly opposed to it.[3]

With members from around the globe, the Eames Commission strove to meet its mandate by offering "guidelines on how Anglicans might live together in the highest degree of communion possible while different views and practice concerning the ordination of women continued to be held within the Communion. . . . Its guidelines are intended to support graceful and charitable relationships and to ensure pastoral care for one another."[4]

In presenting an interim report to the House of Bishops, of the Episcopal Church in September 1989, Dyer said the commission's objective was not to take a position on whether women should become priests and bishops, but rather to encourage ongoing dialogue and prayer among Anglicans with different positions on the issue in the spirit of *koinonia,* a Greek word meaning Christian fellowship.[5] The Eames Commission did not produce a solution to the issue of women's ordination, nor was it intended to. But it did provide avenues for constructive engagement on the issue that eased tensions somewhat in the hope that greater understanding would come in time.

The second commission on which Dyer and Eames collaborated was the Inter-Anglican Theological and Doctrinal Commission. It was also chaired by Eames and became known as Eames II. Appointed in 1994 by George Carey, who succeeded Runcie as Archbishop of Canterbury in 1991, this panel picked up where Eames I left off, examining the issues surrounding the role of ordained women in the Anglican Church, particularly as bishops. As part of its mandate, it analyzed the hierarchy and decision-making apparatus of the Anglican Communion and the theology behind it.

"The Archbishop of Canterbury decided it was critically necessary to establish a doctrinal commission that would lay out for the whole Anglican Communion a theology of church," Dyer said. "It was really the only time a document was written that says 'This is our ecclesiology.' "[6] In its 1997 statement, the commission produced a document that was an attempt to provide a theologically grounded navigational chart to guide the Anglican Communion through the storm-tossed waters of a rapidly changing world that was coming to terms with the demise of colonialism after World War II and sociocultural issues such as the role of women and gays in society. Produced at Virginia Theological Seminary, where Dyer had joined the faculty, it became known as the Virginia Report.

"Some people want to make it sound like the Anglican Communion was a structured, unified thing and then women and gays happened and everything went crazy," said Jim Naughton, who has closely followed Communion affairs for years. "But the Anglican Communion is a relatively young organization. It was really an extension of the British Empire. Once you don't have an empire, once [these churches] are not just branches of the Church of England but are their own churches, then how do they relate to the Church of England?

"That reared its head in the late nineteenth century, but the need to figure that out didn't really hit people across the nose until the end of World War II. It was pretty informal and based on custom and precedent, and clearly that was not going to hold as independence came to many of its former [British Empire] colonies. As a result, Mark was among the leading thinkers about what might be created to supply enough structure, unity, and collaboration for Anglicans but not create another colonial structure or a Roman Catholic structure with strong central authority."[7]

Not only was Dyer a key player in the discussions, he also emerged as the Virginia Report's primary author because of his gift for distilling hours of rambling theological discourse into cogent streams of written words.

"He was very, very good at writing," Eames recalled. "He would go away and the next day we would say, 'All right, Mark, what have you got?' And he would produce it and we'd say, 'That's it!' We would have ended up the previous night in disarray, but by the next morning, he just got it. He had a big yellow pad and this yellow pad used to disappear with him. I used to think he slept with it under his pillow. And he used to scribble away on that pad. But he also had a very good memory. He didn't always have to write. He absorbed things that were going on and then put them on paper."[8]

Eames and Dyer were proud of the Virginia Report, but despite some academic acclaim, it did not have the impact they were hoping

Above left: James M. Dyer and Anna Mahoney Dyer, married in 1926 in Manchester, New Hampshire. *Above right:* Jimmy (Mark), Pat, and Buddy in the famous delivery carriage in Manchester, New Hampshire, 1934

Above left: Jimmy (Mark) with Buddy in Manchester, New Hampshire, 1934. *Above right:* Jimmy (Mark) Dyer at age five, Manchester, New Hampshire, 1935

Above left: St. Anne's Roman Catholic Church in Manchester, New Hampshire, where Jimmy Dyer was baptized on June 21, 1930. *Above right:* The Dyer home at 352 Cedar Street, Manchester, New Hampshire

Jimmy (Mark) with his father, James, and sister, Pat, Manchester, New Hampshire, 1937

On leave at home in Manchester, New Hampshire, after naval training and before heading to Korea, 1952

Petty Officer Third Class Jimmy (Mark), 1952

Two of the Franciscan Sisters at the orphanage in Yokohama, Japan, where Jimmy (Mark) began to sense a call to the priesthood, 1952

The Rev. Joseph "Father Joe" O'Brien, chaplain aboard the *Bon Homme Richard*, U.S. naval base in Yokosuka, Japan, 1952

Priested on August 25, 1963, Mark at St. Anselm Abbey, Manchester, New Hampshire, 1963 (*St. Anselm's*)

Mark with his brother monks at St. Anselm Abbey, Manchester, New Hampshire, 1962 (*St. Anselm*)

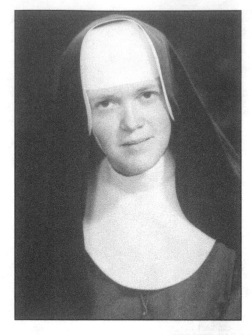

Sister Marie (Elizabeth Hamlin),
Anglican Order of St. Anne, 1970

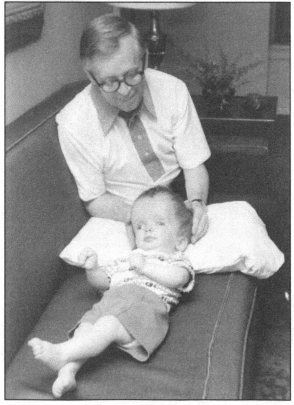

Mark and Matthew,
Boston, Massachusetts,
1972

Mark and Marie Elizabeth on their wedding day, April 17, 1971 in Boston

Mark's study, with icons of Mary, Rublev's *Trinity*, and St. John the Baptist alongside his crozier

Top, middle: Russian Orthodox priest's cross, a personal gift, associated with the Mellennium of Russian Christianity in 1988. *Above left:* Orthodox Medal given to Mark in Cyprus, 1995. *Above right:* Cross of St. Augustine given to Mark by the Archbishop of Canterbury

Above, left: Seal of the Diocese of Bethlehem. *Above, right:* Award of unknown origin.

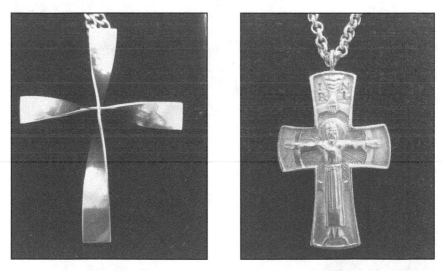

Above, left: Pectoral Cross, Diocese of Bethlehem. *Above, right:* The Lambeth Cross given at the time of The Church of the Triune God presentation, 2007.

Marie Elizabeth and Matthew, October 1972

Mark and Marie Elizabeth with Jennifer (age two), John (age three), and Matthew (age six), Hamilton, Massachusetts, 1979

Christ Church,
Hamilton
and Wenham,
(Episcopal),
Massachusetts

Mark as rector at Christ Church, Hamilton and Wenham, Massachusetts, 1978

Mark with his mother, Anna, and sister, Pat (Cashin), Bethlehem, Pennsylvania, 1987

Mark teaching children in the Diocese of Bethlehem, 1987 (*Diocese of Bethlehem*)

Mark with Geraldine Ferraro at Lehigh University, where Mark received an honorary degree from Muhlenberg College, Bethlehem, Pennsylvania, 1987 (*Tom Amico of Amico Studio*)

Mark with the Eastern Orthodox, including the Patriarch, at a Eucharistic service in Istanbul, Turkey, 1990

Above left: Mark as a faculty member at Virginia Theological Seminary, Alexandria, Virginia, 1996 (*Virginia Theological Seminary*). *Above right:* The Boston Red Sox mitre, Virginia Theological Seminary, 1998

Mark with Virginia Theological Seminary students in the classroom, 1997 (*Virginia Theological Seminary*)

Mark with Metropolitan of Pergamon John Zizioulas, Archbishop of Wales (at the time) Rowan Williams, Ecumenical Patriarch of the Eastern Orthodox Church Bartholomew I, and the Rev. Gregory Cameron in Greece, 1999.

Above left: Mark in Jerusalem, May 1999. *Above right:* Mark and Amy on their wedding day, April 30, 2004, Virginia Theological Seminary

Mark and Amy at Virginia
Theological Seminary
commencement, 2005
(*Virginia Theological
Seminary*)

Above left: Mark reading to granddaughter Ava, 2007. *Above right:* Mark with
Phyllis Tickle, perhaps discussing the "five significant yard sales" of Christianity, at a
conference in Cambridge, Maryland, sponsored by the Episcopal Diocese of Easton,
2010

for. In fact, even a decade later, it had little impact at all, to their dismay.

"The Virginia Report had some legs but not a ton," said Naughton. "It had its critics—people, many from Africa, who wanted a stronger central authority principally in the hands of archbishops of the provinces. But then there were those principally Western folks who said no, we are primarily a confederation of churches. I don't know if the Virginia Report was trying to walk the line between them but [its authors] were certainly aware of them."[9]

In his memoir *Know the Truth*, George Carey, who presided at the 1998 Lambeth Conference as Archbishop of Canterbury, cited the importance of the Virginia Report, "largely written by Bishop Mark Dyer," because it dealt with "the issue of how the Communion arrives at theological truth." But Carey lamented that the report was debated only by one section of the bishops attending the conference rather than by the entire conference. "Thus, the underlying weakness of the Anglican Communion was not addressed adequately," he wrote.[10]

"If you look back at what was drafted in the Virginia Report, you begin to get a sense of how authority is lived in a dispersed way in the Anglican Communion—a rational understanding of it rather than just grasping at straws," said David Hamid, who served as secretary to the commission that wrote the Virginia Report. "I think Mark hoped to give a theological underpinning to our Communion structures. The structures had grown up over the years, sometimes without a theology around them, and he wanted to put that all together somehow.

"I think that the Communion really seriously missed a trick in 1998 by not dealing with the Virginia Report in a substantive way," Hamid continued. "It was circulated as part of the documentation. I don't recall substantive debate and discussion about it at the Lambeth Conference, and as a result, all that work that went into drafting some ecclesiological principles that would help us function as a Communion—well, we lost that opportunity. I'm sure Mark must have been personally very disappointed that it didn't get some traction in the Communion."[11]

The report got a rough reception in parts of the American Episcopal Church as well, where it was seen by some as favoring too much of a concentration of power in the Anglican hierarchy, to the detriment of local dioceses. Dyer never forgot the harsh criticism in some circles. "For some reason, some significant people in the Episcopal Church had a well-planned, well-carried-out plan to destroy the Virginia Report," he said years later. "I don't know why unless someone had a vendetta out for me. I was not going to run around to dioceses like that. The whole thing about the human sexuality issue was all around it, too—at least, that's my idea."[12]

Bishop Rowe said of the Virginia Report, "It was almost summarily dismissed. I think Mark always lamented that it didn't get a fair reading, and it didn't. Mark was trying to get the Anglican Communion to think about what was the function and role of the [pope]. People were just not ready to engage. He raised it but he wasn't asked to raise it. It was sort of beyond the mandate of the report. In retrospect, I think Mark thought that if they had spent more time on the theological foundations of the church, they would have dealt better with the issue of human sexuality."

That didn't happen. "The Virginia Report just got lost. I don't think people read it, and it just went away," Rowe said. "The statement is still there but nobody thinks about those things anymore."[13]

And yet, the Most Rev. Katharine Jefferts Schori, who was elected presiding bishop of the Episcopal Church a decade after the Virginia Report, said that despite the report's lack of impact in the Episcopal Church, "It achieved a level of recognition in some parts of the Communion that was really significant" and contributed to important conversations that took place over the next decade.[14]

Gibaut, a Canadian theologian long active in Anglican Communion affairs, takes the long view on such matters. "No, it wasn't properly received," he said, "but I must say I don't worry too much about these things. The Council of Nicea wasn't received very widely either. It took a good century for that to be received, and so often a text like those texts—it may be that twenty-five years from now, people are looking at it and saying 'Oh my goodness, we didn't even know about this.' "[15]

CHAPTER 11

The Wars of Windsor

I think when I see God, I am going to thank him for sending me to purgatory. It was the worst thing that ever happened to me in my life.[1] —Mark Dyer

B y 2003, powerful crosscurrents were driving powerful forces
toward a powerful collision in the Anglican Communion.

In England, Dyer's friend Rowan Williams had been enthroned
on February 27 as the 104th Archbishop of Canterbury, spiritual
leader of the worldwide Anglican Communion. An eminent theologian and scholar, Williams inherited a fistful of festering religious, social, and political issues that would test the 136-year-old
Communion's ability and will to survive.

Less than four months later, V. Gene Robinson made history of
his own in Dyer's home state. The son of Kentucky sharecroppers
who had become an Episcopal priest, Robinson was elected bishop
coadjutor of the Diocese of New Hampshire. He was the first priest
in an openly gay relationship to become a bishop in the Episcopal
Church or the Anglican Communion.

Neither religious entity had authorized gay priests, much less gay bishops, and predictably, there was a firestorm of reaction to Robinson's election. Some reaction, mostly in the United States and Canada, was positive. But much was negative, especially from Anglican leaders around the world and most especially from Anglican dioceses in Africa and elsewhere in the Southern Hemisphere.

Despite calls from Anglican leaders for the Americans to consult with fellow Anglicans before proceeding, Robinson was consecrated as a bishop on November 2, 2003, in the presence of Presiding Bishop Frank T. Griswold and nearly fifty other bishops. Feelings on both sides of the issue ran high, and Robinson wore a bulletproof vest to his consecration.

The consecration ignited another blast of outrage from other corners of the Anglican Communion. "The devil has clearly entered our church," declared the Most Rev. Benjamin Nzimbi, the Anglican Archbishop of Kenya.[2]

"We deplore the act of those bishops who have taken part in the consecration, which has now divided the church in violation of their obligation to guard the faith and unity of the church," said the Most Rev. Peter J. Akinola, Archbishop of Nigeria and a leader of the opposition to same-sex unions. His statement was issued on behalf of Anglican Primates from the Global South, whom he said represented 50 million Anglicans in Africa, Asia, and Latin America.[3]

Also in 2003, the Diocese of New Westminster in the Anglican Church of Canada added fuel to the growing fire by authorizing worship services to bless same-sex unions, triggering angrier Anglican backlash.

Human sexuality had been on the front burner of the American Episcopal Church for more than a decade. The 1994 Episcopal General Convention had called for serious consultation with the Anglican Communion on the issue. Little consultation occurred, however, until the Lambeth Conference of 1998. There, Anglican bishops from around the world voted 526 to 70 in support of a declaration that "homosexual practice was incompatible with Scripture" and that the conference "cannot advise the legitimizing or blessings of same-sex unions nor the ordination of those involved in same-gender unions."[4]

Despite that admonition, a growing number of clergy and lay members of the American Episcopal Church had begun to call for the ordination of gay clergy and the blessing of same-sex unions. But American Episcopalians were far from united in that cause, and growing numbers of opponents began to seek and find support from Anglican dioceses elsewhere in the world, especially Africa, where the notion of same-sex relationships was anathema to many.

Barely into his first year as Archbishop of Canterbury, Williams was confronted with an existential crisis facing his beloved Anglican Communion. It was clear that African primates, some of whom had ties to the more conservative elements of the American Episcopal Church, would not accept Robinson's consecration as a bishop. It was also clear that as the largely symbolic head of the Anglican Communion without the formal authority of the pope, Williams's options were limited.

But the situation demanded action and Williams acted swiftly. Buying time for cooler heads to do some cooler thinking, he appointed the Lambeth Commission on Communion, a panel of Anglican leaders and scholars from around the world. He gave them a year—until the fall of 2004—to recommend how the "the impaired and broken" Anglican Communion might hold together while resolving profound differences.[5] In hand-picking those who would undertake this incredibly delicate task of theological, cultural, and personal diplomacy, Williams turned to two of his most trusted colleagues, Robin Eames and Mark Dyer.

Williams said he wanted Dyer on the commission "because of that fundamental trust that he knew what the Communion was about. [He was] somebody who . . . I trusted completely to understand the theological complexities of where we were, who couldn't be written off as just a conservative or just a liberal. And there weren't all that many people around at that time in that kind of territory, so that made him all the more important to help focus the real theological soul of the Communion, which I think he did."

Williams called Dyer at his home on the campus of Virginia Theological Seminary and asked him to serve. As Dyer told the story, his first response was, "No, Rowan." But Williams said it was not all that difficult to convince Dyer to serve once more.

"I think he recognized, especially in that wonderfully productive phase at Virginia, that he had a kind of gravitas, a kind of weight, which he could quite properly use," Williams said. "It's a bit like Robin Eames and his situation. And I think still of how fortunate I was to have real elder statesmen like that around to whom one could say, 'I trust you completely to have the interests of the whole Anglican family at heart. I trust you completely to see what the theological issues are going to be.' And that's emphatically how I saw Mark."[6]

In appointing the rest of the body, Williams moved carefully and deliberately to assemble a group that reflected the Anglican Communion's diversity in theology, gender, race, and geography. Dyer was the only American among the eighteen members.

"What was very clear about Mark," observed Gregory Cameron, who served as secretary to the commission and later became bishop of the Diocese of St. Asaph in Wales, "is that he was conservative doctrinally, but liberal socially. You don't see that mix often. There are die-hard conservatives and die-hard liberals. Rowan is another one who has that mix."[7]

The group met three times—twice at St. George's Chapel at Windsor Castle in England, from whence the resulting report derived its name, and once at the Episcopal Kanuga Conference Center in North Carolina—to hear the voices of key Americans, including Griswold and Robinson. "It was very, very hard work, and it was basically about relationships," Eames recalled. "The Windsor Report was brought about in a crisis, which was the threat that the

Anglican Communion would break up. We were asked to find ways to bind it together without suffocating the independence of the likes of America. And there was the whole emergence then of the power in Africa—Nigeria, Sudan, and all those places were getting very, very powerful and of course wanted no truck with women and this, that, and the other thing. So we had a tough assignment."[8]

Cameron remembered Dyer playing a more forceful role in the Lambeth Commission's deliberations than he had in the Anglican-Orthodox dialogue. "I think I saw a slightly more rigorous Mark," said Cameron, who was involved in both talks. "He was aware that more was at stake, that there was more conflict. The Orthodox commission was a common endeavor, but the Lambeth Commission seemed like it was fighting for the soul of Anglicanism.

"There were times when the task seemed impossible. For me it was like walking up the gorge between two cliff faces and as the cliffs got closer and closer together, you felt more and more trapped and that you were coming to a dead end. At the last minute there would be a little chink and you would find a path to go through. At times we thought the Communion would end."

Cameron added, "I have a memory of Mark's voice saying, 'No, no, you can't say that,' and then bringing out academic references, chapter and verse of why you couldn't say that. He had a marvelous ability to search in the stock of his knowledge and bring out a salient fact. What also came through was Mark's loyalty to the Episcopal Church. He was not going to let anybody say derogatory remarks about the Episcopal Church. But in addition, he was quite tough on the Episcopal Church, measuring it against what it could be and what the church was called to be."[9]

While he was defending the American Episcopal Church during the commission's deliberations, Dyer was also keeping the bigger picture of the Anglican Communion in mind, as Williams and Eames expected and trusted him to do. That proved to be a difficult balancing act, even for someone like Dyer who was practiced in the

arts of consultation, compromise, and consensus and an adherent of
the Anglican "Middle Way" between Protestantism and Catholicism.

According to Eames, there was something else on Dyer's mind
that may have influenced his approach to the Windsor deliberations.
As the only American on the panel, Eames said, "Mark was very
troubled that some in the Communion felt the Episcopal Church was
trying to use its political power to influence the rest of us. By that I
mean, the power of the United States in world affairs. He wanted
to separate the power of the Episcopal Church from that image of
America. And I think he felt that we addressed that. . . . He felt he
had a mission to make sure we got the right impression."[10]

On October 18, 2004, the commission issued a ninety-three-page
report with four sections: one describing the state of Anglicanism,
one describing the theological issues that were raised by the current
crisis, one discussing the history of Anglican structure and governance, and one suggesting an architecture of Anglicanism for the
future. Except for the foreword, signed by Eames, the report was
officially a group effort. But according to Cameron, "Mark played a
key role [in the writing] and may have drafted large sections of the
second part and key sections of the third part."[11]

While acknowledging the pain and divisions within the Anglican
Communion, Dyer and his fellow authors strove for a conciliatory
tone, hoping to lower the rhetorical volume of the debate while emphasizing the importance of unity within the Communion. The report
asked Anglicans to be patient, respectful, and understanding of differences in their increasingly diverse church. In his foreword, Eames
invoked the oft-used Anglican catchphrase "bonds of affection"—
this time perhaps more [out of] hope than conviction—to describe
the relational ties that had held the Communion together, and called
the report "part of a pilgrimage towards healing and reconciliation."

The report called for Americans and Canadians to "express
regret" for the distress their actions had caused other members of the

Communion. It asked for a moratorium on the consecration of gay bishops and the blessing of same-sex unions until the next Lambeth Conference in 2008. Conservative bishops were asked not to intrude in the affairs of other dioceses by performing ordinations, confirmations, or other functions typically done by local bishops.[12]

Those recommendations alone would have generated significant pushback in the United States, but many Episcopalians recoiled about halfway through the document when they encountered a recommendation for "a common Anglican Covenant," which would be a mechanism to, among other things, "prevent and manage Communion disputes" by having churches consult with the wider Communion before making certain major decisions. In proposing the covenant, the commission warned, "The Anglican Communion cannot again afford, in every sense, the crippling prospect of repeated worldwide inter-Anglican conflict."[13]

In America, however, the covenant proposal itself ignited more inter-Anglican conflict, as many felt that Anglicans elsewhere in the world could usurp the self-governing prerogatives of the Episcopal Church. The proposal landed squarely on the sore spot Eames had discovered more than two decades earlier—that Americans "wanted to be part of [the Anglican Communion] but they also wanted to maintain their independence," and Dyer had urged an "easygoing understanding" in the relationship.

But the notion of a covenant didn't feel very easygoing to a lot of Episcopalians. For many, the threat of Anglican interference was renewed.

With such strong feelings surrounding the human sexuality issue, the Lambeth Commission on Communion's work had been the subject of much speculation in the church and the press. Apparently anticipating a hostile reception from some of his American colleagues, Dyer issued a defensive statement as the report was released, expressing pride in the document and urging a fair hearing:

The Commission worked diligently over the past year to consider all sides of the issues and to present a fair response to all parties involved. Steeped in Anglican prayer and liturgy, we sought to find a way through the presenting crises to seek the truth of Anglican identity. Those who take time to read the full report will find it to be a comprehensive statement concerning the issues that came before the commission. It treats those on all sides of the issues who have helped to create this division fairly, and asks the provinces and dioceses to cease the actions that are furthering the divisiveness in the church today. Our mission is to seek to serve God and the ministry of Jesus Christ in the world, a task which we can do much better together in unity than we can bitterly divided.

Calling for Anglicans throughout the world to "read, mark, and inwardly digest" the report's contents, Dyer concluded, "In his letter to the Corinthians, who are bitterly divided over similar issues, the Apostle Paul reminds them of their gifted life in Jesus Christ and that they are sanctified and called to be saints. Paul was not willing to break communion with the troubled Corinthians. Let us use his model for seeking unity among ourselves."[14]

Dyer quickly learned that unity was not to be. As he began traveling around the United States to explain and defend the Windsor Report, he encountered skepticism, opposition, and at times, outright anger. After a presentation to a group of clergy and lay leaders, a grim-faced woman approached him. "She said, 'I hope you are ready for hell,'" he recalled. "I said, 'Why?' She said, 'I'm a lawyer, and when a lawyer gets a piece of paper like that on an issue that hot, God help the people who wrote it.'"[15]

Her words were prophetic. While battles over the report raged among Anglicans worldwide, Dyer found himself increasingly under attack in his own country. Many Episcopalians thought the report reflected that Dyer had not supported the actions of the church nor championed the cause of same-sex relationships. They resented the recommendation that the American Episcopal Church should apologize for the pain its actions had caused others in the Communion. Other Episcopalians thought the report went far too easy on the church for its approach toward same-sex relationships, which did not reflect what they considered to be one of the tenets of Anglicanism.

Whatever hopes Eames and Dyer may have harbored that they might somehow be able to help the Communion craft a solution that could hold the fragile coalition together, as they had done in 1994 with the issue of ordaining women, were dashed. "I think it became clear that the compromise that had worked with women's ordination was not going to work in dealing with LGBT issues," said Jim Naughton. "One reason is that LGBT people were understandably reluctant to make themselves visible in much of the world. Nobody could say they didn't know any women, but lots of people could pretend they didn't know someone who was gay, or if they lived in an environment so hostile [to gays] they could say they had never met someone who was gay."[16]

As opposition to the report mounted in the United States, some of Dyer's fellow members of the Lambeth Commission, while still expressing admiration and respect for him, began to wonder why Dyer hadn't given them a better understanding of the traditions, governing structures, and decision-making processes of the American Episcopal Church, especially relating to the limits on the power of the presiding bishop, before they voted unanimously to approve the report. "Mark, I think, was basically trying to craft a very practical Anglican position," Naughton said. "I think there were folks who thought that was fine and good, but if some of us had had a better sense of how the American church made decisions, we might have shaped the report in another way."[17]

Dr. Jenny Te Paa Daniel, who was then principal of the College of St. John the Evangelist in Auckland, New Zealand, was one of those members. Te Paa Daniel, who described her relationship with

Dyer as "a close personal friendship and a deep mutually respectful colleagueship," said that after the commission issued its report, she learned some things she wished she had known earlier.

As Te Paa Daniel recalled, "It was only when I was helped by other Episcopalian friends to understand the historically embedded structural and legal limitations to the power of the presiding bishop that I realized just how scurrilously skewed the narrative around what then Presiding Bishop Frank Griswold 'ought' to have done had become. In other words, the Commission was being led to believe that had the [presiding bishop] acted, albeit precipitously, to inhibit the consecration of Bishop Gene Robinson, then none of the ensuing controversy . . . would have occurred!

"Which of course is patently untrue, but the point is that while all of this nonsense masquerading as 'truth' was swirling around, not once did Mark call it out for what it was. He did not ever say to us that Frank Griswold could no more have stopped the consecration than flown to the moon! None of the other members of the Commission was intimately acquainted with [American Episcopal Church] polity. But you can well imagine that once some of us realized the ecclesiological reality, there was indeed some disappointment that Mark had not thought to enlighten us.

"Now in Mark's defense, of course, none of us as Commissioners was appointed to 'represent' our respective Province or indeed our own Provincial interests, and so it could be argued that in fact, he was not obligated to apprise us of the particularities of the Episcopal Church. But given the circumstances and especially given the level of vilification and outright condemnation of the Episcopal Church on so many fronts, it would have been so much better had Mark thought to lay out the ecclesiological landscape for us right at the beginning."[18]

Te Paa Daniel voiced the same sentiments without naming Dyer in a July 11, 2009, speech to the House of Deputies at the Episcopal Church's 76th General Convention. In remarks that left many of her listeners in tears, she said, "It was only in hindsight as a number of us as commissioners managed to catch our breath, to compare notes, and to consult with our trusted Episcopal Church sisters and brothers that . . . we realized, to our utterly deserved chagrin, that we had perhaps failed, albeit inadvertently, to prevent something of the unprecedented vilification of the Episcopal Church and especially of its leadership that inevitably resulted."[19]

Had she known then what she learned later, Te Paa Daniel said she may have insisted on writing a minority report with several other Commission members. In fact, the Most Rev. Barry Morgan, Archbishop of Wales at the time of the Windsor Report, said that he, Dyer, and Te Paa Daniel seriously considered doing exactly that.

"For some people, the Windsor Report was a kind of fudge but for us sitting on [the commission], I remember there were those who wanted to make it much, much more rigorous and hard, and I remember Jenny and Mark and I saying, 'Look, if that happens, we are out of here. We will write a minority report on this. We can't go along with this.' So in a sense, [the report] was the least worst option," Morgan said.[20]

In the final analysis, Te Paa Daniel said she had no regrets about not filing a minority report. "I came to the realization that it was more strategic and decent of me to trust in [my colleagues'] conviction that while not perfect, perhaps the report was as close to consensus as we were ever going to get," she said.[21]

Morgan added that he fully understood the limited powers of the Episcopal Church's presiding bishop and did not recall other commission members expressing confusion about that. "Mark may well have assumed we knew the score and it may not have occurred to him to explain," Morgan said. "I do not really understand what difference it would have made to the report."[22]

As the debate over the Windsor Report unfolded in the United States, Dyer found himself disagreeing with some friends and colleagues.

"There were aspects of that report that were just tone-deaf," said Bishop Sean Rowe. "The way it was written and the way it approached the issues, I felt like for many of us in the Episcopal Church, it felt like it didn't really fully account for our polity and how we were approaching the issues of the day. And by failing to fully account for and take that into consideration, it felt like we were dismissed. Now it could also be that we were called up short and we didn't like that. So I am willing to own a piece of that. I think history judges those things."

In Rowe's judgment, the Windsor Report never had a chance. "It got into issues that were easy to focus on and then dismiss the rest of the report," he said. "The covenant was dead on arrival. What tanked it was the discipline, the way that constituent members of the Communion could be disciplined. But there's another example of how that issue worked—people didn't consider the merits of the covenant and how they thought it might play out. They just killed it. You are talking about six, seven, eight years of work just going away. I don't want to say this critically, but people were just never going to do it."[23]

The Rt. Rev. Peter James Lee, who was bishop of the Diocese of Virginia when the Windsor Report was issued, said, "The Windsor Report was a nonstarter in my judgment, because one of the great strengths, I think, of the Anglican Communion is that each church of the Communion is autonomous and self-governing, and the Windsor Report would have diluted that autonomy and independence. I think that was really the weakness of it. Mark and I differed about that, but we never broke our relationship over it. Mark, I think, was much more [inclined] toward the Episcopal Church in the U.S. bowing to the concerns of the wider Communion than the Episcopal Church was willing to do."[24]

In the end, the Windsor Report failed to gain the support that might have helped the Anglican Communion find its way out of the painful dilemma over same-sex relationships. Largely cast aside in the United States, the report was not on the agenda of the 2008 Lambeth Conference and Bishop Robinson was not invited to the conclave.

Work was done on developing the covenant recommended by the report, however, and a final draft emerged in late 2009. But by 2017, less than a third of the Communion's provinces had adopted it. To no one's surprise, the province that includes the American Episcopal Church had not approved the covenant.

"I think the impact was not what anybody quite expected and possibly wanted," Williams said. "I think that the vicissitudes around the covenant proposal rather overshadowed the reception and depth of the report. So one can say that part of the legacy—less straightforward, I think—is that the covenant immediately politicized the reception of the Windsor Report in ways which, looking back, I feel drew away from the real significance of what was being done. And yet you'd still find people saying, 'Well, we see the positives there, we accept the positive vision of what we have to rally around, but what the mechanism is to make it work is just too difficult.' "[25]

For Dyer, it was deeply disappointing and personally painful. What might have been the capstone of a long and distinguished career had ended badly and he took a lot of the blame for it.

"Mark, I think, was very pained and very hurt by the reaction and the implicit sense that he was a betrayer of the cause, which was wrong and untrue and unfair," said the Very Rev. Dr. Ian S. Markham, who became dean and president of Virginia Theological Seminary in 2007. "The personal price he paid was considerable. Mark was a very relational person. He was somebody who was proud of the Episcopal Church and it pained him deeply to get such a critical reception. Mark was always the sort of person who had the capacity to understand that not everybody sees the world in the same way that he does. He therefore worked really hard to understand the African perspective or the conservative perspective or the

Orthodox perspective or Canterbury's perspective. There was a sort
of generosity of empathy in Mark Dyer, and that was a difficult place
to be in 2003–2006.

"The fact that they agreed on a report at all is a remarkable
achievement. And there weren't that many people from the American
church who could have done that. Windsor got very bad press in
the American church and a lot of bishops were very critical of Mark
Dyer. But what a lot of critics overlook is what Mark managed to pull
off [which] was that the report in the end treated as equivalent the
American sin of not consulting [with other provinces on the issue
of same-sex relationships] and the African sin of making incursions
into other provinces [namely, the United States]. And that was really,
really important."[26]

The Very Rev. Dr. Martha J. Horne, who was dean and president
of VTS when the Windsor Report was issued, remembered Dyer's
deep disappointment with the reception of the report, especially in
his own country. "I doubt if there was any other time in Mark's vocational life when people questioned his motives or his intentions or
his commitments. But unfortunately, it became almost a loyalty issue
for people," she said. "I think Mark went into that [process], because
of his very, very strong ecclesiology, thinking that this is the family
of the Anglican Communion and we are trying to do what's best
for the Communion. And I think a lot of people in the American
Episcopal Church thought he should have gone in there and been
a complete advocate and mouthpiece—that his first responsibility
was to the Episcopal Church, not to the Anglican Communion. . . .
I think there were some who said in a sense that he betrayed the
American Episcopal Church, and I think for somebody who was as
deeply committed to the church, for there to be any hint or whiff of
betrayal would have been devastating to him."[27]

As time passed, Dyer expressed regret for the pain and disappointment he suffered from the fate of the Windsor Report, but not
for the effort. "In one of his letters, he did tell me that things were

tough with him because of what we had done," Eames recalled. "I think in my reply I asked, 'Mark, do you regret what we did?' And I think the answer came back, 'Not at all. We believed in it.'"[28]

The issuance of the Windsor Report in 2004 and its tumultuous aftermath left the Anglican Communion in a fragile state for the remainder of Rowan Williams's term as Archbishop of Canterbury. Justin Welby succeeded Williams in 2013 and set out to repair the institution's many fissures. The work was often tedious and the results were often incremental. Welby canceled the 2018 Lambeth Conference while he continued to seek greater unity among bishops and commitments that they would attend a conference if it were convened. Anglican Communion veterans in the Church of England, many of whom were friends and contemporaries of Dyer, were pained by the cancellation and said he would have been, too. Yet they expressed hope as plans emerged for a Lambeth Conference in 2020.

"I would hope—and I'm sure Mark would hope—that there will be another Lambeth Conference," said Dr. Mary Tanner, Europe President of the World Council of Churches, who worked closely with Dyer on Anglican Communion affairs. "I'm a great believer in the Lambeth Conference, and I'm a believer also in resolutions being passed at the Lambeth Conference. . . . It's very important to have resolutions so you can live them for the next decade and be accountable for them at the next Lambeth Conference, and then chart the future. I think the Anglican Communion is very important in the total Christian context and in the ecumenical context . . . but the Communion itself has huge challenges about how we hold together."[29]

Dyer's former colleagues agree that were he alive today, he would be right in the thick of things, urging more dialogue and reconciliation. "My guess is that Mark would be an apostle for the unity of the church right now, and whatever Mark's personal feelings were about the issues of the day, he would say the best way to handle them is together and the more divisive we become, the less church we become," said the Rev. Canon John Gibaut.[30]

Former Archbishop of Canterbury George Carey said, "His instincts were always to heal and to bring people together. To him, disunity was not the way forward. If he were alive now, he would not be happy with the state of the Communion and the divisions that exist. He would be wanting to do what he could to reconcile."[31]

"Mark was a classic *via media* man, and I think he would be disappointed by [the] unthinking actions and pressures that come from both extremes in the Communion," said the Rt. Rev. David Hamid, suffragan bishop of the Church of England in Europe. "Whether we stick together as a Communion is a very big question. He would want to have both the theologically conservative people do some serious theological work and he would want the really liberal people to do some serious theological work. He would be urging that from both directions."[32]

"Mark would be deeply grieved and sad. He loved the Anglican Communion not only for the glories of Anglican theology, but also for its legitimate claim to be a worldwide Catholic tradition spanning many cultures and attitudes," said the Rt. Rev. Gregory Cameron. "He would be surprised and grieved by those given to personal invective. Mark was always happy to talk about the issues and happy to debate the theology, but he was never interested in scoring points and denigrating the integrity of those with whom he disagreed."[33]

Rowan Williams offered a somewhat more positive interpretation of how Dyer would view the state of the Anglican Communion as things stood in the summer of 2016. "I think he would have pointed to the sheer resilience of the Communion. It has been much harder to break than a lot of people had thought. It's as though for the last fifteen years, people have been dropping it on the floor with increasing force and it keeps bouncing back. I think he would have appreciated that with a sort of wry smile," Williams said.

"I think he would also perhaps have said that for all the fuss at the margins of certain issues, especially sexuality, what people don't celebrate or register enough is that the theological content of the liturgy goes on working, feeding people, and goes on shaping newcomers into the tradition and new clergy. And my hunch is that being at VTS would have given him that kind of encouragement that in spite of every attempt to derail it, the Communion does its work.

"Because of Mark's monastic formation, there would always be the sense that the continuity is not so much the institution but it's the community at prayer, the community at prayer mulling over scripture together, and although it may be diverted or go underground in some ways, it keeps pushing onward. I think he would have felt that type of confidence."[34]

Barry Morgan, who retired as Archbishop of Wales in 2017, said, "I think he would be glad [the Communion] is in existence and that we just trundle along. Actually, whatever one says about these doctrinal differences, relationships continue; and at the end of the day, you can talk an awful lot of theology about the difference between a federation and a communion and the interchangeability of orders and all that, but it's relationships that actually matter. So I think he would say, 'It's like the church of God has always been—it's a muddle.' "[35]

CHAPTER 12

A Monk in the World

God is not there to be dissected by theologians. God is there to say, "This is who I am, this is what I can do for you, and this is how we can work this out together so you can return to your own holiness."[1] —Mark Dyer

Make no mistake about this. We live our lives by theological vision—our own or someone else's. Making up our minds about our own theology and vision is our only defense against being held hostage by someone else's.[2] —Mark Dyer

You don't have to be spooky to be holy. Not at all. In fact, it's best if you're not. If you are, you probably made it up anyway.[3] —Mark Dyer

Defining Mark Dyer's theology is no easy task.
    Virginia Theological Seminary (VTS) listed Dyer as professor of systematic theology when he arrived, but his approach to theology was anything but systematic. Asked to define Dyer's theology,

nited States and around the world produced

ent of terms, from "three-dimensional" to

" to "Anglo-Catholic with Orthodox ten-

more.

s because he was a walking, breathing ecumenical movement," said James Farwell, professor of theology and liturgy at VTS. "He was Benedictine Roman Catholic in ways that never left him, in my view. He was deeply Anglican, incarnational, sacramental, and he deeply loved and was deeply fed by the Eastern patristic sources. He got the three of them together in his body in a way that I don't think most of us can do. So I imagine you will have to use all those terms to describe Mark rather than trying to sort out which one or two might be the best, because he was a living, monk-in-the-world ecumenist."[4]

While there were many labels for Dyer's theology, there was one universal consensus: he was a Benedictine from the day he entered the monastery until his last day on earth. With its emphasis on obedience, humility, silence, and hospitality, and a daily schedule of prayer, worship, work, and rest, the Benedictine approach to life provided the framework within which Dyer lived and practiced his faith. And through him, it was an example to others.

The Rev. Dr. Helen Appelberg of Galveston, Texas, was so inspired by Dyer's emphasis on the Rule of Benedict during a one-month course she took from him at the Seminary of the Southwest in Austin, Texas, in 1990 that she undertook an in-depth study of Benedictine spirituality. Four years later, she founded the Community of Hope International, a fourteen-week lay pastoral care training program based on the tenets of Benedictine spirituality that has since been adopted by churches across the United States and in Malawi, Africa.[5]

"To me, Mark was the epitome of the Roman Catholic religion, shaped and formed by a Benedictine sense of identity and spirituality, and a generosity therefore of spirit," said Timothy Sedgwick, VTS professor of Christian ethics. "He was Benedictine to the core. You are imprinted by your origins and in this sense, he was a Benedictine, Roman Catholic, Irish Anglican."[6]

"I miss his theological rigor, and that's where I think his Roman Catholic background was a real gift," said Frank Griswold. "Rome is very careful whether you agree with something or not. There are not passionate statements; they are done very rigorously."[7]

Dyer's Roman Catholic academic training at the University of Louvain and elsewhere was rigorous indeed. He was steeped in the thinking of theologians over the centuries, from St. Benedict (who founded the Catholic order named for him) to Thomas Merton to Hans Urs von Balthasar. His wide-ranging studies also made room for many other sources, from the Desert Fathers to Martin Luther to Celtic spirituality to Rabbi Abraham Joshua Heschel.

"Certainly Mark had a broad theological training at Louvain that was filled with the seeds of what became Vatican II. He would have been exposed to all of that," Griswold said.[8]

Although Dyer enjoyed intellectual tussles with his peers, he often seemed to prefer approaching theology from a more practical perspective, using plainspoken terms and simple imagery that made it more accessible to people in the pews. "Mark wore his learning lightly," observed Barry Morgan.[9]

Dyer had no patience with laypeople and even clergy who would say, "Well, I'm not a theologian but . . ." "Ah, but we're all theologians," Dyer would say in his characteristic blend of soft-spoken firmness. "Every time we ask a question about God, we are doing theology."[10]

Rowan Williams saw Dyer's theology as three-dimensional. By that, he meant "somebody who knew what the word 'Catholic' meant" in the sense of the universal Christian church rather than the Roman Catholic Church. "It wasn't the badge of a party and it wasn't the badge of a hierarchical system," Williams said, "but a Catholic theology was one that was really willing to be fed by the widest possible range of tradition and practice without ever being imprisoned by it. And so Mark was always somebody that I thought of as in the center of that stream of theology. And if somebody had asked me to say, 'Well, what does Anglican catholicity mean,' I would have been very tempted to say, 'Ask Mark Dyer' because that's what I mean, that's what it looks like."[11]

Dyer called himself a biblical theologian, a description exemplified by his custom of meeting monthly as bishop with his clergy for Bible study. He loved scripture, read scripture, and studied scripture throughout his life. In his sermons, newspaper articles, and magazine columns, Dyer constantly articulated real-life applications of his theological principles, buttressed by biblical citations and often with challenging directness.

In an October 1994 column in *Episcopal Life*, he wrote: "Wherever the idea that the church's mission is to save souls originated, it did not come from the words—certainly not the deeds—of Jesus Christ. Jesus did not claim to 'save' anyone himself. The sanctuary of the outstretched hands of Jesus on the cross embraced all of us sinners so we might know the incredible love of the God who saves.

"When the church presumes to 'save,' we get dangerously close to acting on behalf of God rather than revealing God. . . . We are not in the business of saving souls. We are in the business of vulnerable and compassionate presence. Our mission, like that of Jesus, is to be a historically situated story of God's incredible love, a story that helps people discover the God who is already in their hearts, in their inquiring minds, and in their longing for true freedom."[12]

In July of the same year, also writing for *Episcopal Life*, he used an everyday image—the yard sale—to analyze change over the course of nearly two thousand years of Christianity. It was a premise revisited by Phyllis Tickle in her 2008 book, *The Great Emergence*. Dyer wrote: "Historically, Christianity has had five significant yard sales. Each one has had to do with the church's struggle to resist the temptation to domesticate God's vision, to settle for change when God seeks transformation. We're clearly moving toward another one. Among the early signs are abandoned large churches in so many of our inner cities, churches where once hundreds and thousands of people worshiped."

Dyer listed the catalysts for what he called the five ecclesiastical yard sales up to that point in history: the ministry of Jesus; Anthony of Egypt, a layman who went into the desert in the late third century to "speak of transformation to a church that had lost its prophetic edge"; the founding of the Benedictine movement in the sixth century where "the gospel was lived with radical simplicity"; the Franciscan Spring of the thirteenth century "when a domesticated church rediscovered its evangelical roots"; and the Reformation in the sixteenth century, when Martin Luther "unraveled the whole church." Dyer noted that the Reformation was the only one of his yard sales led by an ordained person, and he called for the next one—which he said was due any time—to be led by the laity as well.[13]

In 1994, at the request of Presiding Bishop Edmond Browning, Dyer explored his vision of theology in a paper titled, "Doing Theology in a Covenant Community." In presenting it to the House of Bishops at the General Convention of the Episcopal Church in Indianapolis, Dyer told his colleagues:

> We do theology when we embrace our faith tradition the only authentic way we can—with our experience. We do theology when we receive tradition and chew on the biblical record of how our mothers and fathers in the faith heard and wrestled with God's word. We do theology when we attempt to authenticate our own experience of God's presence in our lives by bringing it to the faith community. We do theology when we apply our insights, our own metaphors, our own artful imagination, our own experience to what we have received. We do theology when, in these many ways, our faith seeks understanding. That's what a Middle-Aged friend, Thomas Aquinas, said theology is—faith seeking understanding.

To do theology as Church—as faithful people gathered, seeking an understanding of God and God's will for us—is essentially to compose our life together with God. We are like Martha Graham or Alvin Ailey composing the beauty of a dance. We are like Duke Ellington composing a great jazz symphony. God has given each of us the genius and the command to improvise in ways that no one else can.[14]

In his final address to the annual convention of the Diocese of Bethlehem on December 2, 1995, Dyer issued a ringing declaration of his theological principles, infused with joy, passion, and Benedictine ethos:

I'm leaving with you this morning a radical challenge from the Gospel. It is the challenge to seek God first and always. It is the challenge that finds its origin in the very passion of God's life revealed in the Sacred Scriptures. It has to do with a God whose love for you is so deep that God is willing to die on a cross for us, even for us sinners.

It is the challenge that over fifteen hundred years ago, St. Benedict accepted when he washed his hands of the corrupt Roman culture and went, as he would later put it in his Holy Rule, "to seek God alone so that in all things God will be glorified." What a wonderful vision for this diocese . . . Seek God, alone. Love God, alone. Tell the story of God's love to your children, live the story at home, proclaim it to the ends of the earth, dream about it when you go to bed, let it energize you when you get up! That's our life. Let's not settle for anything less.[15]

Dyer's spiritual life was grounded in prayer. At VTS, he rose before dawn daily and went to his study to pray, worship, and meditate. For hours at a time, he would pray surrounded by his treasured icons, reflecting his deep appreciation of the Eastern Orthodox Church, and often listening to religious music.

Another of his spiritual habits, which several of his colleagues adopted at his urging, was to pray over his calendar for that day—for every meeting, every person, every issue he expected to encounter. He also read the Morning Prayer service, including the scripture passages, before going to chapel because he wanted to hear the Bible readings twice to enhance his understanding of them.

"He had a long list of people—his personal prayer list—that he kept faithfully every day," recalled the Rev. Dr. Katherine Grieb, professor of New Testament at VTS. "There was a time he told me he was praying for me every day, and I didn't doubt that for a minute. There are people who will say that and what they really mean is, 'I am wishing you well at the moment but I really have no intention of remembering to pray for you.' That wasn't Mark. If Mark said he intended to pray for you or he had been praying for you, he meant it."[16]

Years earlier, the Rev. Javier (Jay) Alanis experienced a memorable encounter with Mark Dyer and the power of prayer. Alanis, a Lutheran minister, was a student at the Episcopal Seminary of the Southwest in Austin in January 1990 when Dyer taught a month-long course there to about twenty-five students. "He mentioned in class that he was going to pray for each one individually during the term," Alanis recalled. "He said he would do it by lifting up our face to God—not just saying our name but more like taking our face in his mind and lifting it up to God. And on a certain day during that term, I felt it. I distinctly remember feeling that my face was going up before God, and I intuited that Bishop Mark must be praying for me. When I experienced it, you can't substantiate it—you can only believe it."

In that same course, Dyer spoke openly about another element of his spiritual foundation: his son Matthew. As Dyer was telling the students about Matthew's story and its effect on his own, Alanis said, "I felt the wound in his soul. The only way anyone can really understand compassion is to enter into suffering with another human being. . . . I felt he had done that with his son and in doing that, he had entered into the wound of Christ, because God is found in human suffering. And I thought he understood that existentially, not abstractly."[17]

Many sought to tap Dyer's deep reserves of spiritual insight by going to him for spiritual direction, the practice of working with another to strengthen your faith and relationship with God. It was work that Dyer loved, and for which he received more requests than he could handle. Those for whom Dyer was spiritual director spoke often of his soft-spoken, gentle manner laced with humor that could become quite direct to make a point that needed to be made.

When he became bishop coadjutor of the Diocese of Virginia in 2007, Shannon Johnston began taking spiritual direction from Dyer. He immediately noted some characteristics that set Dyer apart in that role. "A person's spiritual life is like a fingerprint and you cannot do a one-size-fits-all approach. Mark was very highly thought-of as a spiritual director, and I came to understand very quickly that one of the reasons for that was that he made it highly personal," Johnston said. "Mark's style was to explore what made a person tick and why, and he was very searching about that. Unlike most spiritual directors I have encountered or heard about, he was very transparent and shared a lot of his own journey and his own thoughts as a way to stimulate our conversations."

Dyer also had a knack for connecting several seemingly unconnected dots during a lengthy conversation in a way that would refocus attention on a heretofore unspoken issue. "Then you would take off on a very pointed kind of spiritual talk," Johnston said. "Mark as a spiritual director was very big about the integrity of your relationship with God in Jesus Christ, and the presence and nurture of the Holy Spirit in one's life and trusting in that Trinitarian presence in your ministry. He could be very challenging about things when it seemed that you were trusting your own gut to the exclusion of what God might be saying at any given point along the way. He had such a disarming way of being challenging because he would do it with a twinkle and a smile, but there were times when the effect could be really quite straightforward and blunt. But I never felt once that there was something awkward or wrong-foot-forward when he did it. He knew exactly when to do that and why."[18]

Once Dyer firmly admonished a VTS colleague who was complaining to him that she felt like she didn't know her mother anymore because of her Alzheimer's disease. "She is still your mother and she still has much to teach you," he said in a quiet voice that hit home with the force of a hammer. "She will always be your mother and you are just going to have to spend time with her."

"It was not a pastoral pat on the back," the colleague recalled years later, "but he gave me back my mother."[19]

Dyer also put his theology into practice in the churches where he worshiped. Always willing to lend a hand, he would assist in worship services, lead retreats, and speak at forums. "He was theologically conservative but politically very liberal. He said to me once, 'You know, Andrew, you and I are very much alike,'" recalled the Rev. Andrew T.P. Merrow, who was rector of St. Mary's Episcopal Church in Arlington, Virginia, which Dyer attended after arriving at VTS in 1996. "He was clear that everything flows from standing at the foot of the cross, and the strength of the Resurrection allows you to engage the suffering in the world."[20]

Several years later, when Dyer was attending St. Paul's Episcopal Church in Alexandria, Virginia, one of his former students at VTS, the Rev. Judith Proctor, decided that the rabid Boston Red Sox fan needed a very special miter adorned with the iconic "B" from the team logo. And so she made one for him. "He said, 'Judith, I want you to know, I keep it right on top of the TV when they are playing,'" she recalled.[21]

While assisting the St. Paul's clergy at some services, Dyer encountered a theological issue that put him squarely at odds with the Rev. Oran Warder, Dyer's friend and the rector at the time. The issue

was who is eligible to receive Holy Eucharist, or Holy Communion—
only baptized Christians or anyone.

The "open table" issue was especially important to Dyer, who
believed that it was well established theologically that baptism was a
necessary prerequisite for communion. Not only that, it was still the
official policy of the American Episcopal Church, and he was not in
the business of flaunting church rules and doctrine. But many parishes were allowing anyone to take communion, and St. Paul's was
one of them.

"I have always, from day one here, invited everyone to the
Communion Table," Warder recalled. "At some point, it must have
dawned on Mark that I had an open table here. He very quietly
invited me to meet him at the seminary and in his gracious, gracious
way, Mark said, 'You know, I can't be a priest associate anymore at St.
Paul's. I can't be true to what I believe and teach and then worship
in a parish that does the opposite. I'm not going to make a big deal
about this. I just want you to quietly remove my name.'

"It was all spoken in love, very respectfully, but it hurt me
because I loved him so dearly. One of the things I want to be sure to
say is what a wonderful parishioner he was. I'm sure there were times
he had to grit his teeth over some of the sermons he heard and the
liturgy and way it was done, but he was always, always, always gracious. He always found something good to say and never, ever, ever
complained."

True to form, Dyer didn't complain about Warder's open table
policy. He just left.

Months later, he reappeared at church for a Sunday afternoon
service. "He said, 'Put my name back on the roll,'" Warder recalled.
"And then he essentially said that the community was more important than that one issue. It was pure Mark."[22]

CHAPTER 13

Teacher, Mentor, Pastor

It was time to move into a different vocation. I began my vocation as a seminary teacher, and I always hoped and dreamed I would return full circle. This is the answer to a dream.[1] —Mark Dyer

Mark Dyer drove onto the campus of Virginia Theological Seminary in January 1996 pulling a U-Haul trailer behind his car. There was no fanfare, and no trappings of an Episcopal bishop were in sight.

"I remember Martha [Martha J. Horne, VTS president and dean] saying something like, 'Once a monk, always a monk,'" recalled Katherine Grieb.[2]

Eighteen months earlier, Dyer had been one of three finalists for the seminary's top position. The job ultimately went instead to Horne, who was already serving as associate dean. Now he was coming to the campus as a professor of theology and as Horne's first hire. It was a remarkable pairing of two people who didn't know each other until they met near the end of the search process for the new dean.

"I was just mesmerized by him, and I went home that day really knowing I had been in the presence of a holy man," Horne said. "We had a delightful conversation while he was here, and I remember thinking 'Oh my goodness, what a wonderful professor of theology he would be.' That was not to say he would not also have been a wonderful dean, but his vocation as a spiritual leader was clear."[3]

When the seminary had an opening for a theology professor, she immediately thought of Dyer. "Not many people would have done that, especially in her first year as dean," said Grieb, "but she is a strong and kind person, and she recognized that Mark had tremendous gifts to bring to the seminary. Mark was both a humble man and strong in his own way, so neither one of them was afraid to take that risk. . . . I remember that Martha sort of ran the idea by the faculty and said, 'I'm inclined to do this unless anybody has a strong objection' or something like that. . . . Nobody did. I think everyone had been impressed with Mark Dyer. Who wouldn't have been?"[4]

The Rt. Rev. Peter James Lee, then bishop of the Diocese of Virginia, chairman of the VTS Board of Trustees, and leader of the search that resulted in Horne's hiring, said there was no hesitation in hiring Dyer as a professor after he was passed over for the top post. "There was so much interest and support of Mark's unique gifts. I think there was just really gratitude that he was willing to step into that kind of position and not be resentful that he hadn't been offered the top job. But that was really a tribute to Martha Horne as much as to anyone, because she was not in the least threatened by Mark. She saw him as a real addition to the faculty," Lee said.[5]

"For both of them, I think the mission of the church was bigger than their egos or bigger than their ambitions,"said the Rev. Jacques Hadler Jr., director of field education at VTS from 1993 until 2010.[6]

Timothy Sedgwick believes that Horne also saw Dyer as adding to the "healthy presence" of spiritual diversity at the seminary.

"I think especially given his Catholic spirituality and evangelical understanding, including [his] having taught at Gordon-Conwell Seminary, that she was pretty conscious—I know she was because this is one of the reasons I came [to VTS]—of the desire to create a faculty that reflected the breadth of the Anglican Church and the Episcopal Church. And so, that to me is one of the remarkable things about Martha," he said.[7]

By all accounts, Horne and Dyer forged a harmonious partnership. "Mark was a wonderful colleague," Horne said. "There was no friction. It was an extremely cordial relationship. If he felt any tension, I didn't know about it. I just felt there was always a mutual respect for what the other did. He was an easy faculty member, very low maintenance. The only thing I can remember him complaining about in terms of faculty life were the meetings, which we all complained about."[8]

Sedgwick said, "Mark was loyal and faithful and showed fidelity to Martha, and therefore there was a certain reticence at meetings on his part in the sense that he was not going to press a lot of issues. I remember his last faculty meeting and him saying, 'I give thanks for my last faculty meeting.' It drove him crazy because the processing would go on and on."[9]

Notwithstanding Horne's comment that Dyer might have made a wonderful dean for VTS, many on campus who were friends and colleagues of both believe that the role of theology professor was far better suited to Dyer's calling as a teacher, pastor, spiritual director, and mentor. He told the search committee and VTS faculty during the search process that if named dean, he would operate much as he did as a bishop, delegating as many administrative duties as possible and functioning primarily as the abbot of a spiritual community.

"One's mouth almost fell open when we heard him talk about when he was bishop of Bethlehem and his belief in how a system of leadership should run. He was very clear about what his role should be, and there was a kind of awe in the room about it," said Mary

Lewis Hix, then the VTS business manager and controller, who attended the meeting where Dyer spoke to the faculty. "It became very clear to me that Mark was a very holy man and he would be a disastrous dean from my perspective as an administrator. It was no surprise that he was not chosen as dean and to this day, I don't think he would have been happy as dean."[10]

Frank Griswold also thought that Dyer's role as a professor at VTS was ideal for both the man and the institution. "What a perfect influence to have on that seminary campus—that sort of settled Benedictine presence," the former presiding bishop said.[11]

Dyer, then sixty-five, began establishing that Benedictine presence as soon as he started his new life at VTS, the largest of the eleven accredited seminaries of the Episcopal Church. Most of the faculty lived in red brick homes on the eighty-acre, tree-shaded campus in Alexandria, Virginia, and life revolved around teaching, study, and worship.

Marie Elizabeth stayed in Bethlehem, where a support system was in place for Matthew and she could continue her duties as rector of St. Elizabeth's Episcopal Church in nearby Allentown. With their other son, John, and their daughter, Jennifer, also living with her, Marie Elizabeth seldom came to VTS. When Dyer was at his house on campus during the week, he was almost always alone.

"It was a home of sorts for him, but it was really more of a resting place. His true home was with Marie Elizabeth in Bethlehem," said the Very Rev. William S. Stafford, who was Dyer's neighbor on campus. Noticing that the new arrival was often by himself in the evenings, Stafford and his wife, Barbara, began inviting Dyer to dinner.

"We had him to dinner again and again and again. I poured a lot of Irish whiskey down that throat. We would just listen to his stories on and on and on," Stafford said. "We got to know him more and more in a personal way and really became his friends."[12]

When he wasn't in class or chapel or the refectory or reading at home, Dyer often walked the campus, especially in the evenings, and engaged colleagues and students in genial conversation. Just as there are those in the business world who practice "management by walking around," Dyer practiced "ministry by walking around." "He had time for everybody. He would make time to just be with you. That sounds like pretty good theology to me," said the Rev. Mike Angell, VTS Class of 2011.[13]

"Mark was every bit and more a mentor for students," said Horne. "I think that role of mentor to students was really important to him, and it doesn't surprise me because of his Roman Catholic seminary background."[14]

Many former students have stories of encountering Dyer on the grounds and talking about topics that ranged from light and friendly to deep and consequential. Sean Rowe, a student at VTS from 1997–2000, has a vivid memory of one such conversation when Rowe was grappling with the prospect of leaving the seminary. At the age of twenty-two, he was one of the youngest students at VTS and was feeling increasingly isolated among his older colleagues. With his belongings already packed, Rowe headed for Dyer's house one night and ran into the bishop on one of his evening perambulations.

"I told Mark, 'I can't do this,' " Rowe recalled. "One of the things he said was, 'Rather than being formed by a law firm or a corporation or an impersonal organization, you have the opportunity to have your life formed by the church. That is a gift . . . and that is a gift you need to embrace. [If you leave,] you are really taking a gift from God and giving it back. This isn't just about you. It's about God and the community.' Then he got that twinkle and he said, 'This is to be expected.' Now, he would never have said, 'Build a bridge and get over it,' but that's what he was saying."[15]

Rowe stayed and was elected president of the student body. In 2007 he became the youngest bishop in the history of the American Episcopal Church at the age of thirty-two.

In keeping with his commitment to interfaith dialogue and his abiding interest in other religions, Dyer cultivated relationships with students of other faiths and countries. Dr. Salih Sayilgan came to VTS in 2008 as its first Muslim student before obtaining his PhD from the Catholic University of America. "The seminary was very hospitable but the person who made me feel at home the most was Bishop Dyer," said Sayilgan, who is from Turkey. "The way he dealt with me, the way he would talk to me—I would feel like I am not a stranger here. He didn't see me as a stranger because I was a Muslim. In Bishop Dyer, I always saw a very spiritual person who was grounded in his own tradition but also very appreciative of Islam."[16]

Sayilgan took Dyer's class on "The Holy Spirit and the Life of the Church," and one day Dyer asked him to begin the class by demonstrating how Islamic prayers are said. The gesture touched Sayilgan deeply and the two forged a close bond.

"He would always praise my husband to me," said Sayilgan's wife, Dr. Zeyneb Sayilgan, who later became visiting assistant professor of Islamic theology and religious pluralism at VTS. "He was sincerely proud of him in a fatherly way—very proud of his accomplishments. I love the fact that he showed such fatherly compassion, that his compassion knew no boundaries despite our ethnic background. He praised Salih as if he were his own son."[17]

Halim Shukair was born in Lebanon in 1969 and lived through fifteen years of civil war. His parents are Druze, a small Middle Eastern religious sect founded in the eleventh century. The Druze consider their faith to be a new interpretation of the three monotheistic religions: Judaism, Christianity and Islam. He met Dyer in the summer of 2004 at the Canterbury Scholars' Program in England where Dyer was teaching. By that time, Shukair was attending the only Anglican church in Beirut. At a celebration of his birthday on July 29, Dyer handed Shukair an envelope containing an application form for VTS and told the young man that he would help him get a scholarship.

"I cried," Shukair said. "It was such a shock."

Before Shukair could apply for admission, the health of his parents—first his father and then his mother—began to deteriorate and he stayed in Lebanon to care for them for the next ten years. But he never abandoned his dream of attending VTS, and he stayed in contact with Dyer during most of that time. He began working with Dyer in 2012 on admission to VTS, and finally, in August 2015, nine months after Dyer's death, Shukair enrolled to obtain a master's degree in theology, giving all the credit to Dyer. "I pray that the spirit of Bishop Dyer is always giving blessings to the seminary and to me," Shukair said. "I promise him that I will become a priest and a monk just like I told him at Canterbury in 2004."[18]

Dyer also had a strong hand in recruiting the Rev. Joseph Constant to come to VTS, a decision that changed the course of Constant's life and ministry. An electrical engineer working in Boston, Constant had been accepted to another seminary when his father-in-law and rector, the Rev. Paul Schwenzfeier, a friend of Dyer's from the Church of the Holy Spirit in Boston, invited Constant and his wife to dinner with Mark and Marie Elizabeth at Schwenzfeier's home in late 1999.

By the end of the meal, Dyer had convinced Constant to attend a program for prospective students at VTS in February. Constant applied but was told the program was full and that he would be placed on the waiting list. A day after Dyer learned that, Constant was told there was room for him after all. By the time the program was over, Constant and his wife had a new plan.

"We knew what we wanted to do—go back to Boston, quit our jobs and sell our house, and move our family to Alexandria, Virginia," said Constant, who had lived in Boston for fifteen years after moving there with his family from his native Haiti when he was seventeen. "I finally had that sense of stability [in Boston] I had been working so hard for with my wife and infant daughter. We had a nice little house with a white picket fence, and now here was God through Mark telling me I had to leave Boston and go to an unknown place."

It was a leap of faith but Constant took it, graduating from VTS in 2003. Two years later, he returned as assistant to the dean for admissions and community life, later becoming director of ethnic diversity. In 2010, after a massive earthquake struck Haiti, he began working part-time for the presiding bishop coordinating Haitian relief efforts. In 2006, he had launched his own effort, the Haiti Micah Project, which grew exponentially after the earthquake to feed four hundred and fifty children a day, house twenty-seven in an orphanage, build a vocational school, provide clean drinking water for a community, and employ thirty people.

"I would never have imagined that God could use me that way," Constant said years later, still amazed at the turn of events and still grateful for Dyer's support and spiritual guidance along the way. "Knowing that it is the Holy Spirit at work in my life, empowering me to do what I do—I owe that all to Mark."[19]

Dyer came to VTS with the official title of professor of theology and director of spiritual formation. "I thought it was important to do both," he said. "Spirituality has to be considered on the same high level as any other academic discipline. Spiritual formation is essential to doing theology at the highest level."[20]

His courses, on topics such as ecclesiology, sacramental theology, ecumenical theology, "The Holy Spirit and the Life of the Church," and "The Love of Learning and the Desire for God," covered subjects with which he was deeply familiar. He drew on a lifetime of expertise, from the teachings imparted to him as a young Benedictine to his writings on behalf of the Anglican Communion, including its dialogue with the Eastern Orthodox Church.

His classes were almost always full. While his topics may have been appealing, the real draw was Dyer himself—the Korean War veteran and former Catholic monk who became an Episcopal bishop and was on a first-name basis with leading theologians around the world. "With Bishop Dyer, there weren't six degrees of separation. It was more like two degrees of separation from the Queen of England,

Mother Teresa, and anybody who was anybody," recalled the Rev. Canon Jeunée Godsey, VTS Class of 2000.[21]

"I always said that every student needed to take a course *from* Mark Dyer," Sedgwick said. "And I'll say this—every course of his was a course *in* Mark Dyer. In one sense, the courses were very similar, no matter what he taught. It was the powerful expression of the faith of the early church and of the patristic sense of God's presence within our lives."[22]

James Farwell said, "I have heard from students that they didn't take courses because of the topic; they took courses because it was Mark Dyer. They just wanted to be with him. They wanted to get whatever he had to give them."[23]

Much of what Dyer had to give them came in the form of stories. By then, Dyer had decades' worth of compelling tales and he told them in the style of an Irish bard. The details sometimes changed with the passage of time, but the gist remained the same, as did the theological lessons he drew from them.

"I think his courses were full because he was an entertainer. He told stories and the theology was in the stories for him," said Grieb.[24]

"He could have gone into a classroom and read his grocery list and that classroom would have been standing room only," said Shannon Johnston, who became bishop of the Diocese of Virginia in 2009 and who knew many of Dyer's students.[25]

"He was a storyteller, very much in the narrative tradition," said Horne. "Telling stories was really a primary mode of pedagogical instruction for him, and the students loved it."[26]

Indeed they did, and they coined a name for Dyer's classes— "Story Time with Bishop Mark." Yet as much as they loved the stories and the celebrity name-dropping, they also found plenty of substance.

"Seminarians can be a tough audience, but I never in three years or since ever heard anyone make snide or derogatory remarks about Mark Dyer," said the Rev. Bret B. Hays, VTS Class of 2008.[27]

"He had the ability to offer profound insight into the leadership of the church by telling a story so you could get your hands around it," said Mike Angell.[28]

Dyer's method worked just as well outside the classroom. Angell recalled enlisting Dyer's aid when he was fresh out of seminary and trying to organize a "theology on tap" weeknight program for his new parish in downtown Washington, DC. "Mark was going to be my first speaker at this little bar in Foggy Bottom," Angell said. "We had about fourteen people there. I was going to have him talk for fifteen or twenty minutes and then take questions. He said, 'Why don't I just talk about beer and monks?' That's exactly what he did and they loved it."[29]

"He had a real depth. It was presented almost in such a way that you could mistake the depth that was there. That was part of his genius," said the Very Rev. Phoebe A. Roaf, VTS Class of 2008.[30]

"Academics tend to be really in their heads a lot, but he wasn't. There was a depth and an openness that went beyond what you normally see. He knew the head knowledge but he exuded, 'I know this in my heart,'" said the Rev. Wendy Wilkinson, VTS Class of 2004.[31]

"He was clearly a priest first and a professor second," said Wendy's husband, the Rev. Mark Wilkinson, also Class of 2004. "He was teaching out of his love for God, and it gave him a different level of authority from some of the other professors."[32]

The Rev. Dr. Allison St. Louis, VTS Class of 2000, who became director of field education in 2010, was a student of Dyer's. "I think one of the striking things about him in the classroom was his willingness to draw us into conversations with him," she said. "It wasn't a sense that he was this expert passing down knowledge to us. He encouraged us to participate and share our own insights as well, so there was a deep sense of being respected by him and valued by him."[33]

The senior class honored Dyer in 1998 by selecting him as their commencement speaker. He obliged with a stirring address calling the church to transform itself from an inward-focused pastoral community to an outward-focused missionary community.

The students' deep respect for Dyer was coupled with deep affection, which he returned in full measure. Mark Wilkinson said the student body contained a number of what he called "Mark Dyer groupies." At that time, Dyer was the only faculty member who sat with the students in the balcony of the old chapel during worship. In gratitude, they built him a throne of seat cushions.

The Rev. Michael McManus, VTS Class of 2009, remembers students standing and applauding when Dyer would walk into the refectory for a meal. "We loved him so much because he was a good man, a great bishop, and a great person who was always willing to offer a word of encouragement, a good story, or a joke," McManus said.[34]

Perhaps another reason for Dyer's popularity with students was his generous grading policy. "He gave too many A's," said Grieb. "He had trouble giving anything less than an A because he wanted people to feel good about themselves and to feel loved. I remember him saying, 'I just think they're all doing such exciting work.' And I said, 'All of them, Mark?'"[35]

Horne offered another explanation. "Sure they didn't mind getting A's, but they weren't drawn to Mark because he gave them A's. He had a lived theology," she said. "Mark could talk with the students about not only the theological aspects of their vocation and their role as teachers and bearers of a theological tradition, but also about the pastoral dimensions."[36]

Constant echoed that observation, saying Dyer's course on the church and the Holy Spirit made connections for him in a way that many other courses did not. "Suddenly there was an intersection," he said. "You studied all the other courses and read books but this was the heart of the matter. Because Mark lived what he was talking about, suddenly it all made sense."[37]

The appeal of Dyer's classes occasionally fostered resentment among faculty members who sometimes struggled to fill their sections if they were scheduled at the same time as Dyer's. Other faculty found ways to make the system work for them.

"He was immensely popular with students to the degree that if I had an elective that I didn't want to do a lot of work in, I would find it desirable to be scheduled opposite Mark Dyer, because it would guarantee that you would only have four or five people in your class," said the Rev. Dr. Robert W. Prichard, a VTS professor and church historian. "At least some faculty were aware that if you wanted a class with limited enrollment, you could just schedule it at the same time as Mark Dyer's class. Or if you were worried about that, you would go to the registrar and say, 'You can't put me up against Mark Dyer.'"

Prichard also said that although Dyer's streamlined approach to teaching the history of the early Christian church was appealing to many students, it had its limitations. "Mark had a kind of integrated sense of the early church as forming the Christian faith, and he could sometimes speak with a great deal of certainty and authority about what the church says when some other people might be willing to admit that actually this was one of twelve voices in the early church," Prichard explained. "But [this approach] was very attractive to students because it gave them the [understanding] that the sense of the early church is 'A,' and you could absorb that and it would be part of your Christian identity, as opposed to saying they were doing this in Alexandria but they had a different thing going on in Antioch and in Rome, and Carthage seemed to also have some important ideas. So as opposed to the stereo quadraphonic view of the early church, he had a kind of monophonic view of the early church."[38]

In his later years, a standard feature in Dyer's lectures was a stool on which he often sat during class. It came to have a sign on it—"Reserved for Bishop Dyer"—and when it strayed to another room on occasion, his students would restore it to its proper place. "Students really worshiped him," said the Rev. Dr. Judy

Fentress-Williams, VTS professor of Old Testament. "I imagine that he sat on his stool in his classroom and just held court, so there was some awe and reverence around him. I also suspect there were people who didn't agree with him theologically but didn't have the courage to say so out loud. He was so well regarded that it would have been hard to disagree with him."[39]

Dyer knew exactly how he wanted his students to approach scripture. "The scripture is of its nature relational. You don't study scripture to see how Thomas Aquinas unwinds some particular part of theology. You study Aquinas to see what the scripture has said to his heart," he once told his class.[40]

He also knew exactly how he wanted his students to approach liturgy, even though he didn't teach it. "He was a fabulous preacher and liturgist—not in a fussy way but he did have high liturgical standards," said Dr. Ellen F. Davis, an Old Testament scholar who taught at VTS from 1996–2001. "For instance, he didn't want anyone ordained—and I certainly know he didn't want [Marie Elizabeth] to be ordained—until they could celebrate the Eucharist by heart rather than reading it."[41]

And proper preparation for celebrating the Eucharist, through silence and prayer, was essential. "He told us that if we are going to celebrate the Eucharist and we don't prepare ourselves, we might as well die on the way. That's how important it is," recalled Constant. "When someone tells you that, it stays with you."[42]

Dyer also used his classes to imbue his students with his passion for mission. "To me, he had a recurring image of God that made mission not just a task of the church," recalled the Rev. Dr. Richard J. Jones, who taught mission at VTS for twenty-one years. "He had this notion that the love of God overflows and the overflow of God's love is mission. I think that was seminal for him, and I think that's what a lot of students got out of his teaching."[43]

Dyer was cut from a different cloth than any of the other VTS faculty. Although many of his colleagues were ordained, none had his lineage of monk, priest, bishop, and collaborating author of leading Anglican Communion treatises. At the same time, Dyer did not have all the traditional academic credentials of many of his new colleagues, since he did not have a PhD and had not written scholarly books.

"This faculty has always been gracious and they were gracious to Mark, but there were some real pushes and pulls there," said Sedgwick. "Faculty are a strange bunch of people with their own kind of claims of interest and authority, and so they were not always sure what to make of this Anglo-Catholic. Some with evangelical bents, I think, weren't so sure about this Anglo-Catholic spirituality. . . . And we had others teaching theology who had a far more academic sense of wanting to deal with critical interpretation. . . . So there were those tensions."

All of that led to another question—what would Dyer teach? "We had faculty in theology in their own silos with their own interests that made the teaching of foundation courses in theology a challenge," said Sedgwick, who served as vice president for academic affairs from 2007–2013. The solution was to have three basic courses, with each of the three professors teaching one course focusing on one of the persons of the Trinity: Father, Son, or Holy Spirit. Dyer taught the course on the Holy Spirit.

"That's how he settled into his primary interest, which was the doctrine of the Holy Spirit, which really meant the church in its mission and how we understand that in the very nature of the church— how that reflects the divine life, and how that reflects the common communal life and the life that is given in the community of its worship and its order," Sedgwick said.[44]

The results of the three-headed approach to teaching the Trinity by professors of widely varying styles, approaches, and experiences spawned some tension and conflict in the theology department. "There was never a good, cooperative meeting of the minds in that department," said Stafford, who was then the academic dean. "Mark taught theology from a fundamentally Catholic perspective and in

ways that deeply engaged with the Trinity and Christology. All of
that came out of the Virginia Report and in the agreed statements
with the Orthodox that Mark had so much to do with, but that
perspective was pretty nearly alien to his colleagues in the theology
department.

"They were cordial, they were respectful to each other, and we
worked hard to try to get them to be able to team-teach and things
like that, but it just didn't work well. So there was a certain incoher-
ence but also a certain creative diversity in the way in which theology
got taught at Virginia Seminary while Mark was there. I thought it
was wonderful, actually," Stafford said.[45]

The Rev. Dr. Katherine Sonderegger entered this environment
when she joined the VTS faculty as a professor of systematic theology in 2002, six years after Dyer's arrival. She found the dynamics
challenging. Dyer had felt somewhat disrespected as an academic by
some colleagues, she said, because his highest degree was a master's
rather than a PhD. "It took a long time for the department to re-form
and for Mark to have a sense that we regarded him as a full equal,
indeed as a bishop in the church," she added.

Sometimes that authority as bishop surfaced in the classroom.
Sonderegger remembers teaching with Dyer one day when he was
lecturing about the Trinity. "The students were writing down everything Mark was saying," she recalled. "Suddenly he told them to just
stop—he had a good Irish temper and he was angry. He said, 'Close
your laptops, close your notebooks—this is about the salvation of
the world and you can't think this is just some topic like how to clean
the top of your gas range.' I think everybody in the class—I certainly
did—thought that a bishop had just ruled.

"That was something he showed me—that having a deep spiritual life was also about having a fiery passion intellectually but also
morally and ecclesiastically. He was not to be taken lightly. That's
something that was deeply important to me as a colleague and formative to me as a priest. There was no cheap intellectual idea in him."

Another difficult time came after Dyer retired in 2005. Sonderegger said she thought his retirement meant that he no longer wanted to teach any required courses, when, in fact, she came to realize that he did and was hurt when he was not assigned any. It took several years for them to reconcile, Sonderegger said. "I think it was probably a deep wound," she added. "It took a long time for Mark and I to work out our relationship after that. I hope and pray that we did. . . . I deeply loved and admired him—he was a very important person to me."[46]

Dyer was also an important presence in the life of the Rev. Dr. Lloyd Lewis, a campus neighbor and New Testament scholar known to friends and colleagues as Tony. "VTS has a way of producing people who are walking saints, and he was one," Lewis said. At one point, Dyer noticed that Lewis, who was raised in the Anglican-Catholic tradition, drove to an historic Anglo-Catholic parish, St. Paul's Episcopal Church on K Street in downtown Washington, to celebrate the Eucharist at 7:00 a.m. every Tuesday. Dyer asked if he could ride with Lewis, and the two began a weekly custom that lasted for years.

Lewis said the time in the car with Dyer was worth the price of admission alone. "Mark was one of those people who had met all the people who get put in books as footnotes," Lewis recalled. "That was part of this Tuesday morning gig. That's when all of these characters who had floated in and out of his life all just came and sat in the car with us. At least it seemed that way. Mark vividly narrated it all so that these people sort of became our companions."[47]

As one of the very few bishops who had served on the VTS faculty since the institution was founded in 1823, Dyer was a unique presence on campus. Yet he downplayed his ecclesiastical status, wearing the purple shirt denoting his rank only when occasions demanded it.

"He came on the faculty as a full colleague," said Jacques Hadler. "There was no 'I am a bishop or I was a bishop and I know how the church runs—listen to me.' There was none of that in Mark. In terms of age and status, he was way ahead of me, but he related to me as an equal."[48]

"I was always touched by his gentleness, care, and insight, and just utter dedication to extending a view toward the best of the other person," said the Rev. Dr. David T. Gortner, who joined the faculty in 2008 after Dyer had retired. "Here I had a retired bishop for a neighbor and we were just neighbors. That was nice."[49]

Fentress-Williams, who is African-American, remembered something else about Dyer that was very important to her. "He is one of the few white people I knew with whom I felt completely comfortable in my ethnicity because he owned his own," she said. "You knew Mark for six minutes and guess what—he's Irish—good, bad, and unapologetically so. He brought it with him. The way he modeled that invited everyone else—at least in my opinion—to be their authentic selves. And that was a wonderful, wonderful gift."[50]

In a hierarchical church where rank clearly has its privileges, Dyer trod carefully and respectfully, especially where other bishops were concerned. "I don't think Mark played being bishop here," said the Rt. Rev. James J. (Bud) Shand, who succeeded Bishop Lee as chairman of the VTS Board of Trustees in 2009. "He was just part of the staff. But he was certainly a person you could go to for counsel and advice. He was the senior go-to man for all kinds of questions. I know Ian [Markham, dean and president of VTS] went to him about things, and so did I." Students also sought Dyer's advice, which he provided, "although Mark was always careful not to overstep his bounds because he was not their bishop," Shand said.[51]

Describing his own relationship with Dyer as "quite good," Bishop Lee said, "Mark was always very careful never to do anything that was unique to the office of bishop without my advance permission and knowledge—like confirmations or anything like that. In fact, we used him from time to time for things like that and he was very gracious about it. If a church in Alexandria needed to have a confirmation service and the assisting bishop or suffragan bishop scheduled got sick on Saturday night, Mark would bail us out."[52]

Dyer also served as mentor and counselor to at least two new bishops—Shand, who was elected in 2003 as bishop of the Diocese of Easton, which was primarily on the Eastern Shore of Maryland, and Johnston, who succeeded Lee as bishop of the Diocese of Virginia. Shortly after Shand was elected bishop, Dyer asked him if he had been assigned a mentor, as was the custom in the House of Bishops. "They had assigned me a gentleman who was a bishop I knew who shall remain nameless but who was not living in the immediate area. In fact, he was halfway across the country," Shand recalled. "I told Mark who it was, and he said, 'What good is that going to do you when you are trying to meet with somebody?' He said, 'I will try to get you another mentor.'

"So he calls me up later and he says, 'I have a new mentor for you.' I said, 'Who is that?' And he said, 'Me.'" That began nearly three years of bimonthly meetings between the two men.

"I was blessed to have him as my mentor," Shand said. "I would bring up questions or problems or things that were confronting me. He never told me what to do, but he would say, 'Let me suggest that you might try this approach. . . .' He shared his wisdom in a gentle, compassionate, loving way. . . . That was a tremendous gift and something I will never forget. . . . That relationship saved my life in some ways so I didn't make stupid mistakes."[53]

Johnston met Dyer shortly after he was consecrated as bishop coadjutor in May 2007. Dyer became Johnston's spiritual director, advising and counseling the new bishop in sessions spiced with humor and insights gleaned from Dyer's experience. Johnston is named for the River Shannon and his grandmother's maiden name was Ireland, so he and Dyer quickly bonded over all things Irish.

"He was like a guide who helped me out of the gate," Johnston said. "The Diocese of Virginia could not have been more different than the diocese I came from in Mississippi—a small, rural diocese of eighty or so churches and not many more clergy. And I came into a diocese with 180-something congregations and 450 clergy."

Not only that, the Diocese of Virginia was embroiled in costly, acrimonious litigation with a number of parishes that were seeking to leave the Episcopal diocese, maintain possession of their church buildings, and affiliate with Anglican dioceses in Africa. This was largely over issues of homosexuality, same-sex unions, and the ordination of women.

"It was a very steep learning curve and he used that year to help me come into my own and gain some confidence about the kind of bishop I was learning to be," Johnston said. "One of the things I remember that I worked with him on the most was my feeling a little bit disoriented. Now that I am a bishop, could I maintain or even stomach the high theology of being a bishop that I had before? It's like Groucho Marx saying, 'I wouldn't want to be a member of a club that would have me.' Mark really understood that but he didn't give one inch of ground about the theology [of being a bishop]. He called me to embrace that and to know that it happens, warts and all, as long as we go back to trusting God through the power of the Holy Spirit in calling me as a bishop. He kept coming back to that, over and over, and it came to be a great source of feeling like I was back on my rails."[54]

Of all the places Dyer might have ended his ministry, Ellen Davis believes there could not have been a better place than Virginia Theological Seminary. "Did it matter that he didn't have a PhD or a string of publications? No, not at VTS, it didn't," she said. "At other places, he may not have been as effective on the faculty as he was at VTS. I don't mean that he wouldn't have been a beloved teacher, but I think he was at the place where he was maximally effective. And that's both as an Anglican and as somebody forming people for pastoral ministry and for the church's life at all levels of ordained ministry. For the kind of impact that he had, VTS was the absolutely perfect place for him."[55]

CHAPTER 14

Tragedy

I have a very faint memory of Mark's expression of surprise—that he had fed Matthew, burped him, and changed him, and he seemed all right. But then he wasn't.[1]
—Mary Lewis Hix

Mark Dyer's first four years at Virginia Theological Seminary were spent much as he had imagined they would be—teaching, mentoring, providing spiritual guidance, and preaching. There was time for his Anglican Communion work, including a trip to the 1998 Lambeth Conference with Marie Elizabeth and Matthew. And there were weekly drives to Bethlehem on weekends to see Marie Elizabeth and the children. But in 1999, tragedy struck on multiple fronts.

In July, Jennifer suffered life-threatening injuries in an automobile accident in Murfreesboro, Tennessee. After a lengthy hospital stay in Nashville, she returned to Bethlehem in early August for further recuperation.

Shortly after Thanksgiving, Marie Elizabeth collapsed in a camera store in Bethlehem, felled by a cerebral hemorrhage. She never regained consciousness. Jennifer, who was home, took the call from the store's owner and contacted her father, who was two hundred miles away at the seminary. Dyer got the word as he was about to enter a faculty meeting. Ashen, he drove immediately to Bethlehem.

Marie Elizabeth, sixty-seven, was kept on life support for three days, until December 2, while family and friends arrived at her bedside. "Then the decision was made to turn the machines off," said Richard Cluett, then-archdeacon of the Diocese of Bethlehem, who was one of those present. "Mark gathered people important to them in the hospital room to see her off. People prayed and said whatever they wanted. It was very powerful."[2]

Dressed in black clerical garb, Dyer read passages from the Book of Common Prayer with great emotion. "Dad wasn't crying but he was having such a hard time," Jennifer recalled. "We were all there when the nurse unhooked the machines."[3]

Marie Elizabeth's funeral at the Cathedral Church of the Nativity in Bethlehem was well attended by laypeople from her various ministries and from St. Elizabeth's Episcopal Church in Allentown, where she was rector, and by many priests and bishops and a busload of faculty from Virginia Theological Seminary.

"There was a real outpouring of bishops, especially, to go to her funeral in support of Mark," said Bishop Peter Lee, who chartered a plane to transport bishops and staff members for the occasion.[4]

Marie Elizabeth's death shook Dyer to the core. Not only had he lost his wife of twenty-eight years, but he also had become the single parent of three children, one of whom was profoundly disabled and needed around-the-clock care. In addition, John's developmental issues were becoming more pronounced and he continued to struggle with managing his diabetes. After Marie Elizabeth's death, Dyer temporarily moved back to Bethlehem to care for Matthew and John, and to take the extremely unusual step of serving as interim rector at his late wife's church to provide continuity and to help cushion the blow of her loss. He also drove to VTS once a week to teach.

"When [Marie Elizabeth] died, Mark was bereft, not only of her, [and she] was such an incredible energy and power and support in his life, but he was also bereft in dealing with those three kids," said his friend William Stafford. "He did the very best he could, but he had no gift at all for homemaking and didn't really know how to do any of that terribly well. . . . That was a painful weakness for him—at least that was the way it impressed me. It wasn't a lack of love; it wasn't a lack of commitment or concern. It was a lack of knowing how to do it because Marie Elizabeth had done all that."[5]

But if he wasn't an expert in parenting, Dyer was an expert in building Christian community through personal relationships, and he had been doing that at VTS since 1996. He turned to that community for love and support when he moved to campus with Matthew in 2000, and he found both in abundance.

He had spoken so openly about Matthew with colleagues and students that many in the community felt like they knew his son, even if they had not seen him in person. And they certainly knew what Matthew meant to Mark. So the VTS community responded with open arms. Whether it was staying with Matthew day or night, or cooking meals, walking the dog, running errands, or supporting Dyer in any number of ways, people answered the call.

And they didn't wait to be called.

Ellen Davis often took the Sunday morning shift. "It was my habit to go to early church, and so afterward I would go over to his house and spend the rest of the morning with Matthew so Mark could go to church and be active in the life of a parish," she recalled. "It was such a tender, loving relationship. . . . He would often talk about Matthew and Matthew's story, but he did it with pride and I don't think Matthew's limitations were a burden to him. He felt Matthew's life was pure gift. I remember him saying Matthew has this wonderful effect on people because he has never had a moment of anxiety in his life. His presence is suffused with peace."[6]

But just as Dyer's new support system was restoring a sense of equilibrium to his life, another blow fell. On September 8, 2001—a quiet, sunny Saturday afternoon on the VTS campus—Mary Lewis Hix, who was then the seminary's vice president for administration and finance, was in her office on the first floor of the administration building, from which she had an unobstructed view of Dyer's house. Glancing up from her computer, she saw emergency vehicles with flashing lights pulling into Dyer's long driveway.

"My first concern was actually that it was Mark," Hix said. "I immediately left my desk and went running down there, and they were carrying Matthew out. I think he was dead at that point."

Matthew's heart had stopped beating, and he died in Dyer's arms.

Hix accompanied Dyer and a friend to the hospital, where a helpful Baptist chaplain found a Book of Common Prayer from which Dyer read prayers and scripture passages for Matthew as he had for Marie Elizabeth twenty-one months earlier. Matthew Dyer, whose life expectancy had been as little as three months, had lived nearly twenty-nine years.

Later that afternoon, as news of Matthew's death spread, members of the VTS community began to gather at Dyer's house. "He was so happy to see people come and be here with him. There was this sense that the community was arriving, and that was feeding him," Hix said.[7]

Matthew's funeral service at the seminary, in the presence of the VTS community, family, and friends, was a poignant scene. "There was this old man, and the son he had taken care of for his whole life dies," said the Rev. Canon Blake Rider, VTS Class of 2004. "People handle something like that in different ways. They go into the fetal position or drink themselves into oblivion. But there was Bishop Dyer, attending the burial office and loving his son in death as he did in life. It was a stunning thing."[8]

Not long after Matthew's death, a student sitting next to Dyer in the chapel balcony during a worship service noticed that Dyer had not joined in reciting the Nicene Creed as he always did. "When I asked him about it," said Mark Wilkinson, "he said, 'Right now I can't say it. I need you to say it for me.' "[9]

And he did.

CHAPTER 15

New Life

In October of 2003, while Mark and I were deepening our friendship and exploring something more, we attended an ordination to the priesthood of six people, one of whom was Mpho Tutu, daughter of Archbishop Desmond Tutu of South Africa, who preached at the ordination. Mark and Desmond had been friends for years. As we left the church, Mark said, "I want to introduce you to Desmond." I went with Mark to the receiving line. Mark and Desmond embraced and spoke of the joy-filled day. Mark then said, "Desmond, I want to introduce you to a colleague of mine at the seminary, Dr. Amy Gearey." As I received a warm embrace from the archbishop, he asked Mark over my shoulder, "What else, Mark? And what else?" Mark responded, "Well, maybe a lot more." They exchanged wonderful smiles, and Desmond Tutu wished us much happiness, a taste of what was to come.[1] —Amy Dyer

One of the faculty members who offered to help with Matthew's care when Dyer moved back to campus with him was Dr.

Amelia Gearey (known to all as Amy), professor of Christian education and then director of the Center for the Ministry of Teaching.

She first met Dyer when he came to campus to lead a Quiet Day
in the early 1990s. "I don't remember what he said, but I do remember a sense of his presence. And I thought to myself, 'This is a very
holy man,' " she said.[2] They encountered each other again in 1994
when he met with the faculty as part of the dean selection process.
After he came to VTS in 1996, they became colleagues, serving on
committees and working on projects together.

In the spring of 2001, Dyer faced increasing parental responsibilities when John, unable to manage life on his own in Pennsylvania
with his medical and developmental difficulties, moved into Dyer's
home at VTS. About that same time, Dyer needed someone to stay
with Matthew once a week while he taught an evening class. Amy
volunteered. She had not met Matthew, so on the first night of class
she went to Dyer's house not knowing what to expect.

"Matthew was upstairs on the couch, and Mark said, 'We'll
know right away if he likes you or not,' " Amy recalled. "I said, 'That's
pretty scary,' and he said, 'Oh no, I'm sure he'll like you.' When I
went upstairs, I said, 'Hello, Matthew,' and Mark said, 'I can tell he
likes you already because he's calm.' "

When Amy asked how she should spend her time with Matthew,
Dyer told her to just sit with him. "I remember sitting in the chair
and I just had this strange feeling like I'm ignoring Matthew. So I
went over to him and sat on the floor and I just talked to him. It was
just as natural as anything to sit there and talk to Matthew," she said.[3]

Amy met John while she was caring for Matthew in the evenings.
With her background in education, she realized that John had cognitive difficulties and in time, she became involved in his care as well.

By the fall of 2003, Amy and Mark often found themselves grabbing early lunches together in the refectory because of their teaching
schedules. Their friendship deepened during these daily exchanges,

and in late October, Dyer asked if she would like to go to the movies one night. She said yes.

Amy's birthday followed soon thereafter. She had a gift certificate, to a fancy French restaurant, that was about to expire, and she asked Dyer if he would like to go with her. Yes, he said. They shared a long evening of quiet conversation as he regaled her with stories about growing up in Manchester, the navy, the monastery, and leaving the Catholic Church. That evening was soon followed by another dinner and movie. By then, they were holding hands as they walked to the theater, where they encountered some students from the seminary. Word of their budding relationship quickly spread, and Dyer moved from the chapel balcony to sit with Amy at ground level for worship services.

Pleased with these romantic developments, Dyer helped spread the news himself. "I remember when Mark and Amy started dating," said Judy Fentress-Williams. "He said to me, 'I'm seeing someone.' I said, 'Oh, really.' Then he told me who it was. I was so happy because it was clear that he was not only happy but he had a happiness he wanted to share."[4]

Their courtship settled into a comfortable pattern. On Saturdays, they would drop John off for a movie and then take a walk or go for a drive. Later, they would share a pizza with John at Mark's house. On Sunday nights, Amy would fix dinner at her house, where she introduced Mark to classic radio shows like *Gunsmoke* and *Yours Truly, Johnny Dollar,* and they listened to Big Band music.

After church one Sunday, Amy drove Mark back to campus before leaving to visit one of her daughters for Thanksgiving. She said, "Before he got out of the car, he said, 'So, you'll think about marrying me?' And before that, he asked, 'Do you know how old I am?' [He was then seventy-three and she was fifty-six.] I said, 'Yes,' and he said, 'So you'll think about it?' And I said, 'Yes, I'll think about it.'"

That was as close to a formal proposal and acceptance as it got. Amy and Mark kept in touch by phone over the holiday, "and when I came back, it was just assumed that we were going to get married," she said.

Then one Saturday morning in February 2004, Mark appeared at her door sporting aviator sunglasses and a ski jacket. Before he arrived, Amy had received a very clear signal about him. "I don't know if I had been praying or what but something just came to me and said, 'You have to be with this man because he has more work to do, and you've got to be there to support him,'" she recalled. The thought was prescient, because at that time, Dyer was working on the Windsor Report and the Anglican-Orthodox dialogues.[5]

As it turned out, Mark had a plan of his own for that Saturday. Instead of taking a walk, he took her to a jewelry store and bought her an engagement ring.

Bud Shand, a good friend of the couple, was on campus not long afterward for one of his mentoring sessions with Mark when he learned that a wedding was in the works. " I came in and sat down in his office and he said to me, 'Now look, when you're done here today, I want you to go see Amy.' I said, 'Sure, no problem.' Halfway through, about an hour and a half later, he said, 'Now look, when you're done, I want you to go see Amy.' I said, 'I know, you already said that.' Then he said to me at the end of the time, after some closing prayers, 'Now, don't forget,' and I said, 'I know, you want me to go see Amy.' Then I said, 'What's the matter—are you in love with this woman? Why don't you just marry her?' In fact I said, 'I think you're going to marry that woman. I can see it in your eyes.' And he kind of got a little chuckle and a twinkle, and he said, 'You better go see her.'

"So I went to see Amy and as I walked in, she said, 'Did you see Mark?' I said, 'See him? My God, he couldn't stop talking about you. I think he's in love with you. I suggest you ought to marry him.' And she said, 'Well, we are.' "[6]

Mark wanted to get married in Ireland, but arrangements proved too complicated. So the ceremony took place at VTS on April 30, 2004. The newlyweds took a three-day trip to St. Michael's, Maryland, on the Chesapeake Bay, but the real honeymoon came that summer—three weeks at Canterbury in England where Mark was teaching, and two weeks exploring the west coast of Ireland.

That summer, Amy moved into Mark's house on campus and they started building their new life together. A big part of that life would be John, who had been diagnosed in the early spring of that year with a form of autism. Doctors said John would probably never be able to live on his own, and indeed, he lived with Mark and Amy for most of their married life.

Mark retired from the faculty in December 2005 (he continued to teach as an adjunct professor until 2014), and even though there was still church work to be done, there were also trips to take and grandchildren to spoil. First came a trip with Amy to Cyprus in the spring of 2005 for the last meeting of the Anglican-Orthodox dialogue. But when they arrived, there was one small logistical issue. He was the only bishop who arrived with his wife, to the mild consternation of his Orthodox friends. The solution? The American couple was packed off to a dormitory, giving Dyer another story that he would tell many times with glee. They traveled to London several times in the coming years, including for the official presentation of the final report of the Anglican-Orthodox dialogue in January 2007.

Later in 2007, they returned to Ireland for three months while Amy took a sabbatical on Celtic spirituality. There was another vacation trip to Ireland in 2010. As always, the visits touched Mark's soul. "He said the minute he stepped on shore he felt at home," Amy said. "He didn't feel at home in Manchester as much as he felt at home in Ireland. I think he would have liked to have stayed. If there had been a parish open, I think he would have taken it, and I was ready to stay with him."[7]

But there were strong forces pulling them back to Virginia, including Mark's new extended family—Amy's daughters Robyn and Amanda, and Robyn's children, Ava and Sam, who were six and three in 2010. Stepfather and grandfather were new roles for Mark, but he embraced them wholeheartedly and was embraced in return.

"I think he definitely did enjoy being a granddad," said Robyn. "They were the only grandchildren he had, and he was always really great with them—very loving and very kind. Mark was the first visitor I had at the hospital when Sam was born. The children called him Papa and there was a lot of fondness and good memories."[8]

"I always felt like he considered me one of his daughters," said Amanda. "He didn't meet me until I was twenty-two years old, but he was always genuinely proud of me when I did something, and that just made me adore him even more. He was always very supportive of me."

Dining out with her new stepfather was simple and predictable, Amanda recalled. "He was happy going to an Irish pub for dinner, even if the food wasn't really that good. But he was always really excited to go, so you really didn't care and you just went to whatever Irish pub he wanted to go to. Most likely he would have fish and chips and a beer," she said.[9]

There was also time for Dyer to ramble around the campus with Hobbes, his dog and constant companion. The two were fixtures in the life of the VTS community.

By all accounts, Dyer's unexpected romance and marriage brought him new levels of happiness and harmony as he entered the last decade of his life. Faculty and students at VTS remember the couple strolling the campus hand in hand and sharing their joy freely with others.

"It seemed to me that marriage No. 1 was the kind of marriage that a former monk and a former nun would have," said his fellow professor Robert Prichard. "They were deeply connected to one another, but they seemed to have no trouble living parts of their lives quite separately from one another."[10]

In contrast, said William Stafford, who administered the wedding vows to Mark and Amy, "Amy's love for him and his love for her was wonderful. And the home they had together was as welcoming and as gracious and loving as could be imagined. I am so deeply moved by what they had together. . . . It seemed to satisfy parts of him that were hanging out and lonely. Amy didn't do it all—she helped him do it—but it was a wonderful gift and a wonderful transformation and so healing for them both."[11]

CHAPTER 16

Journey's End

I remember about a year before he died, when Bishop Dyer was visibly deteriorating and I think he was aware of his fragility, he brought up a story about one of the brothers in the monastery, who he said officiated at one of the services one day, then went back to his seat in the chapel and died. "Now, THAT'S the way to go," Bishop Dyer said.[1]
—The Rev. Christopher H. Miller

The first sign of health issues came in 2008. Amy and Mark had been married for four years when a PSA test as part of a routine physical indicated prostate cancer. Too old for surgery, he underwent the implanting of radioactive "seeds" in his prostate, which proved highly successful. At the same time, he was diagnosed with celiac disease, which hit the Irishman as hard or even harder.

"He would always say, 'I am the son of a baker and I love my bread!' " said Amy.[2] So she set out in search of gluten-free bread and beer, determined to find a new supply chain for two of his major food groups. One of her prize discoveries was a recipe for gluten-free blueberry muffins, which they made every weekend and he devoured. And he found a couple of gluten-free beers that passed his taste test. But try as he might, Mark found it hard at times to stay gluten-free.

"The only irritation I remember was over his gluten-free diet. [Amy] was the enforcer of the diet and he never wanted to do anything to hurt her feelings," Robyn recalled. "But when he came to our house to be with the kids, we'd indulge him and order pizza, and he'd check the fridge to see if I had any [non-gluten-free] beer."[3]

Mark's strength returned and during the summer, while Amy worked long days as associate dean of students, he proudly cooked dinner every weeknight. It was basic fare—chicken, meatloaf, spaghetti, fish, hamburgers—but he was happy to prepare it for her.

In July 2009, he came through a knee replacement without serious complications and soon was feeling good enough to travel again. He and Amy sometimes took their grandchildren to the second home they had purchased on the Potomac River in Southern Maryland, where Mark enjoyed swimming with the kids and eating ice cream on warm summer evenings.

More trouble came in the fall of 2011 with the discovery of three blocked arteries in his heart. Doctors performed an emergency triple bypass and implanted a pacemaker. He came through rehab in good shape and was active again.

But in February 2013 he went to the doctor with back pain and a cough. A CT scan showed tumors on his spine. A month later, when he was at home dressing for a doctor's appointment, Dyer suddenly couldn't walk. The diagnosis this time was multiple myeloma—a very serious type of cancer of the plasma cells of bone marrow.

After undergoing radiation treatment and physical therapy, Dyer could walk again. Next came chemotherapy, and he continued to improve over the summer.

About that same time, just when Mark and Amy needed it the most, help finally arrived for John in a form that was nothing short of a miracle. Amy remembered the details vividly. "For nine years through the social services networks in the District of Columbia, Virginia, and Maryland, I looked for help and support for John. I spent hours on the internet looking for homes that could provide care for him. We hired a company to help us. After four months of work, they were unable to find any source of help. The company declined to bill us, but their representative had one suggestion: 'Go back to the City of Alexandria and speak with a caseworker whose name is Liska.'

"I was willing to try but was afraid that this, too, would fail. Liska told John and me, 'If we can't find help, then the system has failed.' For a year, she and I talked almost weekly. She was always available by phone, email, or text. She got John qualified for Medicaid and approved for a state grant. In March of 2013 [when] Mark was diagnosed with cancer, I called Liska to tell her. In April, she called to say she had found a place for John. She was with us every step of the process, and we moved him into his room early in June 2013. The next day, I called Liska to thank her and tell her it had gone well. She wasn't there. Her phone was disconnected, her email came back, and the text went nowhere. I tried to find her, but she had vanished. It was like the old TV show, *Touched by an Angel*, when the angels come, do what needs to be done, and disappear."[4]

By the end of the year, things were looking up and the Dyers spent a couple of weeks in Florida early in 2014. But as the year progressed, he began losing ground and by late summer, the chemotherapy was no longer working.

There were trips to the emergency room in August and October as his condition worsened. The final visit to the oncologist came in October, when the decision was made to discontinue chemotherapy. As they were driving home, Mark patted Amy's hand and said, "You're going to be alone. I don't want to leave you alone."[5]

Even as his strength failed, Dyer was determined to teach his weekly fall class, "The Church and the Holy Spirit." The first class was on September 4. Frail but beaming, Dyer was there, perched on his stool and ready with his stories. But first, he leveled with his students.

"I've got multiple myeloma. It's been working on me for two years, and it's a great test," he said.[6] Asking for their prayers, he cited a passage from Job, the long-suffering figure from the Old Testament, saying it was very helpful to him. The class met for two hours. Dyer filled most of that time himself in his familiar style, blending scriptural citations with Anglican doctrine and references to other faiths and, of course, stories of his personal experiences. But as each week passed, the class took more and more of his fading energy.

On September 25, Dyer spoke to his students again about his health. "I have very serious cancer and there is no way of getting out of it," he said. "Chemotherapy eats your thoughts before you get a chance to think them through, and I find it very frustrating. So be patient, please."[7]

It was the last time he saw his students. Faculty colleagues took over the class for the rest of the semester.

With Dyer now seldom able to leave the house, family and friends came to him, whether to bring food or Holy Communion or conversation or prayer or just presence.

One frequent visitor was Christopher H. Miller, a VTS student who had been in spiritual direction with Dyer for a year. Miller had met monthly with Dyer in their previous relationship; now he visited Dyer weekly to read Morning Prayer with him. "He would be lying on the bed and I would be sitting on a chair next to the bed, and he would sort of doze in and out of sleep and I would just keep going," Miller said. "Once I was halfway through the creed and he just woke up and joined in. The words of the daily office were inscribed in his heart in such a way that they informed all that he did and all that he was. . . . To literally and figuratively sit at the foot of his bed and learn from him in that way remains the greatest gift I could have ever asked for from him."[8]

Another who came often was Shannon Johnston, who also had experienced spiritual direction with Dyer. Now Johnston came as friend, colleague, and bishop. "When the last illness settled in, before he was less cognitive, we had one particular conversation about end-of-life issues," Johnston recalled. "I thanked him for everything he had meant to me and to the church that I loved. He was one of the most consequential figures of the Episcopal Church in my lifetime. He didn't stop me when I praised him, as he usually did. I think he knew it was important for me so I could say goodbye.

"I remember telling him, 'Do you remember when I was a new bishop and you kept asking me, "Do you trust God?" Now it's my turn to say to you, "Trust the mystery."' His eyebrows went up and he smiled. I think he liked the term but more importantly, he understood what I was saying. I didn't want to go into explicit death talk. It was inexplicit, but I meant it in terms of the death journey and Mark understood it that way."[9]

Three days before he died, Mark and Amy were home alone, waiting for the night hospice nurse to arrive. Mark's head was clear, and Amy asked him if he remembered his days in the navy as young Jimmy Dyer during the Korean War. Yes, he said.

"Were you afraid to die?" she asked.

"No," he said. "I was never afraid to die. I had a job to do and I was just doing my job."

"Are you afraid to die now?" she asked.

"Jesus Christ is my Lord and Savior and I am not afraid to die," he said firmly.[10]

"I can't imagine anyone more equipped to say that," Rowan Williams said when he heard of Dyer's declaration.[11]

Death came while Dyer was at home, surrounded by family and friends, at 5:15 p.m. on Tuesday, November 11, 2014. It was Veterans Day.

CHAPTER 17

Legacy

In the last analysis, I have always believed, it is not so much their subjects that the great teachers teach as it is themselves. —Frederick Buechner, *Listening to Your Life*[1]

Mark was a scholar, first of all, and a teacher. Not all bishops are. —Presiding Bishop Frank T. Griswold[2]

There was no greater spiritual teacher than Mark Dyer. —Bishop Sean Rowe[3]

In a crypt in the magnificent edifice of St. Paul's Cathedral in London lies Christopher Wren, one of the great architects of his—or any—time. Buried in one of his most famous and enduring creations, Wren's epitaph reads, *Si monumentum requiris circumspice*, or "If you seek his monument, look around you."

The thoughts of Martha Horne, former dean and president of Virginia Theological Seminary, went immediately to that inscription when she sought to describe the legacy of Mark Dyer: "Look at the lives and vocations of all the students who were touched and formed by him. Look at the larger legacy within the Anglican Communion and the Diocese of Bethlehem, his presence in the House of Bishops, his contributions to ecumenical dialogues—it's a quite strong and generous and positive legacy, both on individuals and on systems."[4]

There are many ways to take the measure of a person, and Mark Dyer was a man of many dimensions—monk, priest, bishop, pastor, preacher, teacher, theologian, ecclesiastical diplomat, leader of ecumenical and interfaith dialogues, son, husband, father, stepfather, grandfather, friend, and tireless advocate for the poor and marginalized. The foundation of it all was his faith and a deep and abiding sense of spirituality. Many would say that the most frequent manifestation of his many gifts came in the form of teaching, whether in classrooms with students or in Bible study with parishioners or clergy, in mentoring seminarians, priests, and bishops, in leading retreats, in providing spiritual direction and in modeling values of Benedictine spirituality that went back fifteen hundred years.

In her sermon at Dyer's funeral at St. Paul's Episcopal Church in Alexandria, Virginia, on November 20, 2014, Horne observed, "Mark was a wonderful teacher, and he loved to teach. He wasn't partial to fifty-minute lectures, although he was perfectly capable of giving them, but he preferred to teach as Jesus taught: by telling stories. He also taught by the example of his life. During the craze of 'What would Jesus do?' bracelets, I remember our students asking, 'What would Mark Dyer do?' "[5]

"I think his legacy was very much connected with the person he was," said Ellen Davis, who once co-taught a class with Dyer at VTS. "He was one of those people who is remembered as a great teacher—and I don't just mean a classroom teacher or even primarily a classroom teacher—but as a model of church leadership. I have a colleague who spoke to me of him as his model of what a bishop ought to be. I think he was a pastoral bishop, and we have not so many of those in the church."[6]

"I would say a whole generation of VTS students will understand the relevance of the Trinity and Christology to the mission of the church and the life of the church in an unrivaled way because of Mark Dyer," said William Stafford, another former VTS colleague.[7]

Two other close associates of Dyer listed integrity and humility as key elements of his legacy. Shannon Johnston cited Dyer's "inspiring integrity in all things" as one of his hallmark characteristics. "You could not be around him, even casually, without knowing you were in the presence of someone great, and his humility added to that," said Johnston, comparing Dyer to Desmond Tutu in that regard. "Mark didn't take himself so seriously but he took everything he was committed to in complete seriousness."

Johnston also cited spiritual direction as another area in which Dyer had considerable impact in guiding and shaping generations of clergy. "So many people were touched by him in this way, and his willingness to make himself available for that was extraordinary. Even when he wasn't feeling well, he would find a way to make it happen," he said.[8]

"I think his legacy is the need for intellectual honesty and integrity in not sweeping difficult intellectual facts under the carpet or pretending that the scriptures are anything other than the word of God but interpreted through human hands," said Barry Morgan, former Archbishop of Wales. "I can't remember who it was who said that for every difficult problem, there is an answer that is simple, straightforward, and usually wrong, but that's something Mark would certainly have appreciated."[9]

"He had the mind of a scholar and the heart of a pastor," said retired VTS professor Lloyd Lewis. "His was the story of a person who was, in a lot of ways, unsung in terms of the popular knowledge. But nonetheless he was one of the people who [was] deeply influential in making the wheels turn. I don't think anything could completely capture who he was in the corporate memory of the church and who he was in his ministry."[10]

Assessing Dyer's contributions to the Episcopal Church, former Presiding Bishop Frank Griswold said, "Because of his formation, particularly as a Benedictine within the Roman Catholic Church, he brought with him a kind of depth and wisdom in the area of community life and theological reflection that I would say deeply enriched the life of the Diocese of Bethlehem and the House of Bishops and his work with international missions. These were profound gifts to us."

In a more personal observation, Griswold added, "He had this kind of monastic sense and I think some people found him a little distant and remote. And I think he was drawn more toward people who shared some of his sensibilities theologically and liturgically than he was to some others. He could sense kindred spirits who would more naturally be his friends and those who would appreciate the complexity of things rather than simpler answers. Rigorous theological explorers were much more his allies than those who, in his mind, quickly reduced things to right and wrong categories."[11]

On the Anglican Communion side of the ledger, Dyer left a body of work for which he will be well remembered, as well as a great number of lasting relationships forged during good times and bad. "I think the legacy of Mark lies in a number of different ways," said George Carey, who retired as Archbishop of Canterbury in 2002. "It seems to me that he came with a certain number of gifts, and those gifts were exploited very positively—the gift of teaching, the gift of analysis, the gift of being a very good theologian. But he was also gifted in terms of personality—very warm and approachable with the ability to communicate. So all those gifts enabled him to be the right person at the right time to take things forward—with the Orthodox, with the Catholics, and particularly with our internal unity. We didn't have anyone else quite like that. Rowan Williams would have had the capacity to do it, but not with the personality and the down-to-earth-ness that Mark had. It's also a typical American way, so he worked the crowds, you know. He was good at articulating a vision, but he was equally good over a cup of coffee."[12]

The ability to connect with people was a skill Dyer used intentionally and it lay at the heart of his effectiveness, said Johnston, a
close follower of Anglican Communion activities. Dyer was proud
of the work he helped produce for the Anglican Communion,
Johnston said, "but it was always punctuated by that work being
accomplished through relationships rather than through committee
dynamics. He spoke about it in very personal terms, and it was clear
that he could make things work because he would always make a
point of finding what to like about somebody. That was the way he
could turn the wheel. That was very important to Mark because it's
relational. He did not believe that ecclesiastical politics happened
in a vacuum, especially not in the Anglican tradition. . . . Whenever
there was a task to accomplish, it would start with how he was able
to make a relationship turn and that would produce the work—not
vice versa."[13]

Others saw Dyer's Anglican Communion legacy through different lenses. "Bishop Dyer was a gentle, affirming, caring human being
with an inbuilt moral compass pointing in the direction of ubuntu.
His appreciation of our interdependence, that we are made for each
other—God-carriers all, none superior, none inferior, and none
more or less titled—inevitably placed him on the righteous side of
church discussions on contentious issues, the side of the disregarded,
marginalized, ostracized, and oppressed," said Desmond Tutu, the
South African Nobel Laureate and Anglican Archbishop Emeritus
of Cape Town.[14]

Tutu's successor, Njongonkulu Ndungane, said, "Bishop
Dyer was God's gift to the church in general and to the Anglican
Communion in particular. God endowed Bishop Mark with a very
rare combination of gifts as an astute theologian with a penetrating
mind, a sensitive pastoral heart, and a deep spirituality. My experience of him was of a person whose 'eyes of the soul' were fixed on
God for guidance, direction, and sustenance whilst his 'ears of the
heart' were attentive to God's voice."[15]

"Mark's legacy, I think, is a classical Anglican legacy—that is, a pursuit of moderation, a pursuit of reasonableness, a pursuit to be knowledgeable of the rock from which you have been hewn," said Gregory Cameron, who watched Dyer at work for years during the Anglican-Orthodox dialogues and in the writing of the Windsor Report. "Perhaps because of Mark's journey from Catholicism, I had this sense that he was dismayed by absolutism, when others were unwilling to see another view and would not accommodate difference. Mark might have a view that said, 'This is the best answer we can have for now. This is our working hypothesis; this is what our knowledge leads us to believe. Let's keep exploring.' "[16]

Robin Eames, Dyer's valued colleague and collaborator, said Dyer's frequent role as the only American in the room during deep and delicate discussions of theology and diplomacy put him in a unique position to help foster understanding through extensive dialogue driven by his conviction that solutions could be found to the issues at hand.

"It was vast," Eames said of Dyer's influence. "His legacy as a person was that he understood the American view of government. He was able to translate that into the wider thinking of Anglicanism, and his contribution was to influence us through the sheer weight of his personality, that here was someone who believed that there was no such thing as the unanswerable problem when people of good faith talked and prayed together."[17]

"At a time of tremendous mistrust in the American church, he brought a voice to the councils of the Anglican Communion that was respected, and that was a rare voice in those days," said the Rev. Dr. Roger Ferlo, retired president of Bexley Seabury Seminary, who served with Dyer on the VTS faculty. "In that way, his great contribution at the time was that he could be a bridge between factions in the Episcopal Church, but he could also affect the way the Episcopal Church was being regarded by the larger church."[18]

"I think the work he did was to give us a theological understanding of what our Communion of churches is like and should be
like, and how the instruments that serve that Communion should
be understood—how we need to understand legitimate exercise of
authority in the church," said Bishop David Hamid. "He was willing
to propose on sound theological principles the issues that the Anglican
Communion has always found itself to be a bit allergic to. . . . What is
the authority of an Archbishop of Canterbury? What is the authority
of the Primates? What's the authority of the Anglican Consultative
Council? What is the authority of the Lambeth Conference?

"These are the kinds of things that Mark was pushing us to
reflect on seriously, because I think he was convinced—and he certainly convinced me—that unless we understand those things, we
are not going to be able to deal with conflict and with challenges to
our Communion. So in a way, he was trying to prepare us theologically to deal with issues and tensions as they arise."[19]

Dyer's two principal efforts in that regard, the Virginia Report
in 1997 and the Windsor Report in 2004, fell short of that goal. But
some say their ultimate influence is yet to be felt. "He left an abiding witness in the Windsor Report and the Virginia Report," said
Stafford. "Even though some aspects of [those] are being rejected or
treated as if they are secondary, they are just too powerful to dismiss
altogether. I think they will be a continuing legacy to the church.
Even though the reports did not succeed, the underlying theology is
just too powerful within the church and will continue to be. Some
people will try to ignore it but they won't be able to ignore it with
complete success."[20]

Rowan Williams, who worked with Dyer on Anglican Communion
issues for more than twenty-five years, and who still keeps a photo
of Dyer in his study, saw traits and skills in his American friend that
were equally valuable in all aspects of his ministry. "He was someone
who would call the Communion to its better self," Williams said. "I

think that's what his contribution was at every level. It was a contribution made through all the commissions that he was involved in, but a contribution also made through the seminary, which has an extraordinary position in the Anglican world, and Mark was near the heart of that, spreading that influence out well beyond the Episcopal Church and well beyond the Anglican world, too, because that is something he cared a lot about.

"There was also that extraordinary and inspiring and focusing work as a teacher for people around the Communion. That's probably the hidden stream in the story, a more unobtrusive but equally real contribution. People have seen and heard somebody for whom this Anglican identity makes that kind of sense. He had that kind of depth."[21]

Jim Naughton, a longtime observer of Anglican Communion affairs, said Dyer was uniquely equipped for the work he undertook for the Communion. "He had a sense of how a changing traditional institution had tried to deal with new intellectual trends and world events and how it needed to study its insensitive self and reform itself," Naughton said. "He had been through that in the Catholic Church and he went through it again in the Anglican Communion. He was in some ways an obvious choice to be on the international panels that looked into those things. He was also such a reassuring presence—not just in a 'there-there' sort of way, but in a 'Here is what we know and here is how we bring what we know to an attempt to reconcile [our] differences' sort of way. He was gifted in that. He really was regarded as one of the people who helped think through how the Anglican Communion should structure itself so it would have some degree of unity."[22]

"He came into the Anglican Communion at a time when Robert Runcie could say the Communion was held together by bonds of affection," said the Rev. Canon Samuel Van Culin, a longtime top official of the Anglican Communion and graduate of VTS who worked closely with Dyer. "There was a lot of rumbling beneath the surface, but we were able to hold it together and Mark played a large role in articulating, supporting, and helping the Anglican Communion do that."[23]

One of Dyer's great passions was interfaith dialogue, as evidenced by the seventeen years he spent painstakingly shepherding the Anglican-Orthodox talks. He lived to see the successful conclusion of that with the publication of *The Church of the Triune God*, but by the time of his death, much of the energy and commitment to those dialogues that meant so much to Dyer and the Anglican Communion compatriots of his generation had begun to wane.

The era began with dramatic hope in 1966 when Pope Paul VI placed his ring on the finger of Archbishop of Canterbury Michael Ramsey. They had just announced the beginning of a dialogue between Anglicans and Catholics following the first public meeting between men in those positions since the Reformation. But it all came to a quiet end with the beginning of the new century.

"That generation was really ready for those conversations," said Sean Rowe. "They were way far along. Mark was in it at the right time, and he was able to be part of it. But that wave crashed on the beach and those ecumenists are all gone."[24]

Nevertheless, said Ian Markham, dean and president of VTS, "Bishop Mark Dyer is undoubtedly one of the great church leaders of his generation. Steeped in a rich, informed theological outlook, heavily shaped by Orthodox theology, he was a scholar, a pastor, an ecumenist, a global interlocutor, and a very good bishop. Most importantly, he was a man of prayer who loved to engage with the text of scripture. He touched so many lives with his grace, wit, and erudition. His crowning achievements are many: he played an important role in keeping the Anglican Communion connected with the Orthodox churches after the ordination of women; he sought to be a peacemaker at a difficult time for the Anglican Communion with his service on the Windsor Report; and he was the supreme representative in the House of Bishops of a Christian scholar committed to full inclusion of women and LGBT people grounded in his convictions as an incarnational and Trinitarian Christian."[25]

Yet while Dyer played a leading role as some of his era's headline-grabbing religious issues unfolded, his most profound and most enduring legacy was far more fundamental than any of that. "He was someone who shaped the faith of others by the depths of his own faith," said Ellen Davis. "It was a very compelling witness—just the way he lived his life, not any particular point that he was trying to make—just the self-effacing joy with which he experienced life, including its difficult parts."[26]

Said William Stafford, "I think I can speak for probably two-thirds of the people you have interviewed for this book in saying that one of his legacies is just his tremendous impact on me. I'm a more faithful Christian because of knowing Mark Dyer."[27]

ACKNOWLEDGMENTS

I t all started with a dinner invitation in the summer of 2014. My wife, Dorothy, said Amy and Mark Dyer had asked us to join them for a meal in their home on the campus of Virginia Theological Seminary. Dorothy, who had worked with Amy at VTS for some time, knew them well. I had gotten to know Amy and, more recently, had encountered Mark at various campus events and found him to be warm, gracious, and brimming with fascinating stories from his life, which he related with relish, glee, and humor. And there was a buzz about him—something about a Korean War vet who became a Catholic monk and somehow ended up as an Episcopal bishop. The invitation sounded like a very pleasant way to spend a summer evening, and it was. But little did I know where it would lead.

It turned out that in addition to dinner, Amy and Mark wanted to talk about a book. She had been encouraging him to write one, and now seemed like the time. They were looking for a collaborator and asked me if I would be interested. I said I would and asked him what kind of book he had in mind. "I don't want a biography," he declared. "I want a book about my theology."

To me, a lifelong layman who was faithful in church attendance but thought theology was territory reserved for professors, priests, bishops, and archbishops, this sounded like a daunting task. More accurately, it seemed like an impossible task.

Thankfully, Amy had another take on things, and she gently steered the conversation in that direction, pointing out that because Mark had lived his theology in remarkable and inspiring ways, it was virtually impossible to separate the two. Then my news instincts, honed over forty years in journalism, kicked in and I think I said something profound and profane like, "Not only that, your life would make a helluva story."

Thankfully, again, it was an easy sell, and we agreed to set to work before summer's end. As it turned out, we had far less time than we thought. Mark's multiple myeloma, which had been held in check by chemotherapy, came roaring out of remission and this time, it couldn't be stopped. We had about six weeks of interviews— one per week—and Amy got me assigned as the teaching assistant in Mark's weekly class at VTS, where I could see him interact with his students and hear even more of the stories he told about his life and ministry. All of this personal exposure to Mark was extremely valuable, but it all stopped by the end of October, and on November 11, 2014, he died.

Once again, Amy was determined to press on even as I explained that the project had now become much more of a research undertaking, finding documents to read and people to interview from Mark's past. As a journalist, at least I had some inkling of how to go about this, and the work continued.

So first and foremost, thanks go to Amy Dyer, without whose generous support and vision and indefatigable determination this book would not exist. Not only was she a valuable research partner who opened doors from Saint Anselm Abbey to the House of Lords and snagged interviews with the top brass in the Anglican Communion, her discerning eye as a reader was also most helpful.

Mark's and Amy's families were also incredibly helpful. Mark's nephew, Jimmy Cashin, and his wife, Alynn, opened their home to Amy and me on our research trip to Manchester, New Hampshire, in 2015, told us many family stories, and gave us a tour of the family home and the neighborhood where Mark grew up. Mark's sister, Pat, was also a most gracious source of information during a visit to her residence in Hampton Beach, New Hampshire, the seaside town visited by the Dyer family every summer while Mark was young. Mark's children, Jennifer and John, shared vivid recollections of family life. Mark's niece, Kathleen Henderson, and foster daughter, Victoria Hutchinson, also provided helpful information and insights. Amy's daughters, Robyn and Amanda, shared stories of their experiences with Mark in his later years, and Robyn doubled as a careful and thoughtful editor for the manuscript.

Of the one hundred and four people interviewed for this book, each and every one provided a valuable piece to the puzzle that was Mark Dyer. And I am especially grateful to the many who went above and beyond in sharing their time, memories, insights, records, and suggestions, as well as for their willingness to tell unvarnished truths.

At Virginia Theological Seminary, special thanks go to Ian Markham, dean and president, for his very generous support and encouragement, his keen analytical eye and sense of history, and his willingness to sit for a very long interview and do some very basic theological tutoring of the author. His predecessor, Martha Horne, who hired Mark Dyer, also provided valuable information, insight, and wisdom.

Other helpful contributors from the VTS community are far too numerous to name here. You will find them throughout the book. But I would be remiss if I did not thank and salute Tim Sedgwick, Bob Prichard, and James Farwell for observations and perspectives that helped keep me on course. The same goes for two former VTS faculty members, Ellen Davis and Bill Stafford.

Three bishops in the VTS orbit—Shannon Johnston, Peter James Lee, and Bud Shand—were most generous with their time and willing to supply some deeply personal interactions with Dyer. And two former presiding bishops of the Episcopal Church, Frank T. Griswold and Katharine Jefferts Schori, contributed enlightening insights.

Bishop Sean Rowe is in a category by himself for several reasons. First, he observed Dyer from different and valuable perspectives over time. Not only was he Dyer's student at VTS, but Dyer became his mentor as a priest, and Rowe later served as interim bishop in Dyer's former diocese in Bethlehem, Pennsylvania, where many of Dyer's associates were still in place. Even more valuable to the author, Rowe was willing to undergo repeated rounds of questioning and to serve as a sounding board.

On the research front, expert assistance was provided at VTS by Head Librarian Mitzi Budde and Archivist Christopher Pote. Shelagh Casey Brown, director of alumni and church relations, was a key source of both information and patience with repeated inquiries. At the national level, Mark J. Duffy, canonical archivist and director of the Archives of the Episcopal Church, was a most valued source of vital information.

There were also very helpful sources at stops along the way of Dyer's ministry. In Manchester, the abbot of Saint Anselm Abbey, Mark Cooper, provided documents from monastery files and patiently explained the workings of the church and the Benedictine order and how they related to Dyer's leaving both. In Hamilton, Massachusetts, longtime parishioner David Bergquist spent the better part of a day sharing material from the church archives and from his own archival memory bank. And to my amazement and gratitude, he cheerfully answered follow-up questions for the next two years. Dean and Gail Borgman shared many memories of Mark, Marie Elizabeth, and the children during a long, languid summer afternoon at their home and a waterfront restaurant. Titus Presler taxed his encyclopedic memory and analytical powers to produce detailed, insightful interviews by phone and in person.

In Bethlehem, Pennsylvania, Dyer's former staff mobilized to produce reams of records and materials, and to undergo extensive interviews covering his time as bishop and their roles and recollections. Heartfelt thanks to Rick Cluett, Bill Lewellis, Scott Allen, and Bob Wilkins, not only for what they initially supplied but also for the rounds of follow-up questions and data collection that ensued.

In the realm of the Anglican Communion, where Dyer is widely remembered and respected, there were many key contributors to this effort who were interviewed on two trips to the United Kingdom. Amy and I jointly interviewed Rowan Williams, Robin Eames, Barry Morgan, John Gibaut, and David Hamid. On a separate journey, Amy interviewed George and Eileen Carey, Gregory Cameron, Walton Empey, and Mary Tanner. The Anglican Communion Office staff, especially Christine Codner and the Rev. Terrie Robinson, received us warmly and provided critical information both then and later. Jenny Te Paa Daniel supplied thoughtful and detailed responses to emailed questions, corresponding with us from Aitutaki, her beautiful island home in the South Pacific. Desmond Tutu and Njongonkulu Ndungane offered their valuable insights from South Africa.

There were also many valued colleagues and friends who helped shepherd me through this process as a first-time author. Craig Thompson was there at the beginning, offering encouragement and sage advice on writing and legalities. Thanks to Mike Bowler, who has been showing me the way since he was assigned to break me in as a cub reporter on *The Atlanta Constitution* in 1970 and who found plenty to fix, macro and micro, in my drafts of this book. Thanks to longtime friend and newspaper associate Fraser Smith, who provided encouragement and erudition over many breakfasts. Thanks to Chris Eddings, my former publisher at *The Daily Record* in Baltimore and the most voracious reader I know, who read every word of every chapter, flagging the good stuff while extracting motes the size of logs from my eyes and asking laser-focused questions over countless cups of coffee. Tom Kunkel, former dean of the journalism school at the University of Maryland and later a college president, was a source of calm practicality and expertise at just the right time on just about everything. Jim Naughton had been there before, as a newspaperman turned author, and he knew the pitfalls, not to mention the DNA of the Diocese of Bethlehem and the Anglican Communion. Ed Miller knew how to navigate the U.S. military history establishment, which I didn't even know existed. Tom Horton told me to keep it simple (so much easier said than done, my friend), Del Wilber told me to keep it real, and John Frece told me how to organize a project like this one. David Folkenflik deconstructed the research and writing process for me, and Will Englund gave me the long view of how to approach something that had seemed almost unapproachable. Peter Meredith was always there with a knowing chuckle and the patience to answer endless questions about endnotes. And special thanks go to Sharon Ely Pearson, my editor, and the dedicated team at Church Publishing Incorporated.

Thanks to my son, John, and daughter, Nancy, for asking just enough questions about the progress of the book to keep me encouraged, not discouraged. And most important, thanks to Dorothy, my wife since August 25, 1973, an accomplished writer in her own right and the foundation of our family, whose quiet, steady support made all of this possible. Aside from noting that Bishop Dyer seemed to have taken up residence in the spare bedroom, she was an amazingly good sport about the whole thing.

Tom Linthicum
Alexandria, Virginia
June 2017

NOTES

Abbreviations:
MD is Mark Dyer
VTS is Virginia Theological Seminary

Chapter 1

1. MD, interviewed by the author, October 7, 2014.
2. http://nhpr.org/post/when-mills-ruled-manchester-amoskeag
   -manufacturing-companys-legacy#stream/0
3. MD interview.
4. Ibid.
5. Pat Cashin, interviewed by the author and Amy Dyer, July 25, 2015.
6. Ibid.
7. Ibid.
8. As told to Amy Dyer, undated.
9. Pat Cashin interview.

Chapter 2

1. As told to Amy Dyer, undated.
2. U.S. Navy records.
3. Ibid.
4. Ibid.

5. http://www.navalaviationmuseum.org/attractions/aircraft-exhibits/item/?item=f9f_panther
6. U.S. Navy records.
7. United Press, "Carrier Planes Blast Red Bases in Biggest Raid," undated.
8. Associated Press, "Red Power Plants at Chosin Razed," July 5, 1952.
9. MD, interviewed by the author, October 7, 2014.
10. Ibid.
11. Ibid.
12. Thomas Merton, *The Seven Storey Mountain: An Autobiography of Faith* (New York: Harcourt, 1948), 402.
13. MD interview.

Chapter 3

1. MD, interviewed by the author, October 7, 2014.
2. Ibid.
3. Ibid.
4. Ibid.
5. Ibid.
6. MD, interviewed by the author, September 9, 2014.
7. "USS *Bennington*: Ship's History: December 15, 1941–December 31, 1955," Department of the Navy, 25.
8. U.S. Navy records.
9. Letter of December 22, 1958, from Father Thomas F. Maloney to the Very Rev. Christopher G. Hagen, O.S.B., Saint Anselm Abbey.
10. MD, interviewed by the author, September 30, 2014.
11. Saint Anselm Abbey records.
12. The Rev. Peter Guerin, O.S.B., interviewed by the author and Amy Dyer, July 27, 2015.
13. Former Presiding Bishop Frank T. Griswold, interviewed by the author, February 13, 2016.
14. Saint Anselm Abbey records.
15. MD, interviewed by the author, September 2, 2014.
16. Ibid.
17. Ibid.
18. MD, class lecture at VTS, September 4, 2014.
19. Ibid.
20. The Rev. Mark Cooper, O.S.B., interviewed by the author and Amy Dyer, November 18, 2015.
21. Father Martin Mager, interviewed by Amy Dyer, April 21, 2017.

22. Jimmy Cashin, interviewed by the author and Amy Dyer, July 25, 2015.
23. MD interview, September 9, 2014.

Chapter 4

1. MD, interviewed by the author, September 9, 2014.
2. David Miller, "Memoirs of a Draft-Card Burner," *Reclaiming Quarterly,* Spring 2001, reclaimingquarterly.org.
3. Rosalie G. Riegle, *Crossing the Line: Nonviolent Resisters Speak Out for Peace* (Eugene, OR: Cascade Books, 2013), 85.
4. MD, interviewed by the author, September 2, 2014.
5. Ibid.
6. Ibid.
7. Tom Roberts, "Former Catholics Finding Home in Episcopal Church: For Two Ex-Priests, Bethlehem Diocese a Haven," Religion News Service, March 19, 1992.
8. The Rev. Dr. Helen Appelberg, interviewed by the author, March 16, 2016.
9. Letter of December 31, 1970, from MD to the Rt. Rev. Gerald F. McCarthy, O.S.B.
10. Ibid.
11. The Rev. Mark Cooper, O.S.B., interviewed by the author and Amy Dyer, November 18, 2015.
12. The Rt. Rev. Sean Rowe, interviewed by the author, January 6, 2016.
13. Former Presiding Bishop Frank T. Griswold, interviewed by the author, February 13, 2016.
14. MD interview, September 9, 2014.
15. Ibid.

Chapter 5

1. MD, class lecture at VTS, September 11, 2014.
2. Pat Cashin, interviewed by the author and Amy Dyer, July 25, 2015.
3. Kathleen Henderson, interviewed by the author and Amy Dyer, July 25, 2015.
4. Jimmy Cashin, interviewed by the author and Amy Dyer, July 25, 2015.
5. Henderson interview.
6. MD, class lecture at VTS, September 11, 2014.
7. Archives, Anglican Church of Canada.

8. Eileen Carey with Andrew Carey, *The Bishop and I: Taking the Lid Off the Church's Best-Kept Secret* (London: Hodder and Stoughton, 1998), 32.

9. Letter of December 31, 1970, from MD to the Rt. Rev. Gerald F. McCarthy, O.S.B.

10. Michael Hamlin, in-person and telephone interviews with Amy Dyer, undated.

11. Victoria Hutchinson, interviewed by the author, June 15, 2016.

12. Diocese of Massachusetts records.

13. The Rev. Paul Schwenzfeier, interviewed by the author, January 19, 2017.

14. Diocese of Massachusetts records.

Chapter 6

1. MD, class lecture at VTS, September 11, 2014.

2. Jimmy Cashin, interviewed by the author and Amy Dyer, July 25, 2015.

3. MD, class lecture at VTS, September 11, 2014.

4. Ibid.

5. The Rev. Dean Borgman, interviewed by the author and Amy Dyer, July 28, 2015.

6. MD, class lecture at VTS, September 11, 2014.

7. Eileen Carey with Andrew Carey, *The Bishop and I: Taking the Lid Off the Church's Best-Kept Secret* (London: Hodder and Stoughton, 1998), 32.

8. MD, class lecture at VTS, September 11, 2014.

9. Ibid.

10. John Dyer, interviewed by the author and Amy Dyer, October 3, 2015.

11. Jennifer Dyer, interviewed by the author, October 16, 2015.

12. Kathleen Henderson, interviewed by the author and Amy Dyer, July 25, 2015.

13. Borgman interview.

14. The Very Rev. Martha J. Horne, interviewed by the author, January 10, 2017.

15. Borgman interview.

Chapter 7

1. MD, class lecture at VTS, September 4, 2014.

2. Archives of the Episcopal Church, Resolution No. 1976-AO69.

3. Trinity Episcopal Church website, www.trinitybridgewater.com, church history timeline.

4. David Bergquist, interviewed by the author and Amy Dyer, July 28, 2015.
5. https://www.hamiltonma.gov/about/
6. Elizabeth B. Webber, *On This Rock: A History of Christ Church of Hamilton and Wenham* (privately published: undated), 5.
7. Ibid., 11.
8. MD, interviewed by the author, September 23, 2014.
9. Bergquist interview.
10. Ibid.
11. Ibid.
12. The Rev. Dean Borgman, interviewed by the author and Amy Dyer, July 28, 2015.
13. Diana Butler Bass, *Strength for the Journey: A Pilgrimage of Faith in Community* (New York: Church Publishing, 2017), 56.
14. Ibid. 56.
15. Ibid, 59.
16. The Rev. Dr. Titus Presler, interviewed by the author, November 18 and 21, 2016.
17. Ibid.
18. Bergquist interview.
19. Webber, *On This Rock*, 14–15.
20. MD interview, September 23, 2014.
21. Bergquist interview.
22. Webber, *On This Rock*, 52, 58.
23. Bergquist interview.
24. The Rev. Paul Schwenzfeier, interviewed by the author, January 19, 2017.
25. MD, lecture to VTS community, March 19, 1996.
26. Borgman interview.
27. Bergquist interview.
28. Gail Borgman, interviewed by the author and Amy Dyer, July 28, 2015.
29. Presler interview.
30. Episcopal News Service, "Central New York Tags Orlando Dean Whitaker," November 13, 1980.
31. Bergquist interview.
32. Webber, *On This Rock*, 25.
33. Bass, *Strength for the Journey*, 71.

Chapter 8

1. MD, interviewed by the author, October 7, 2014.
2. MD, interviewed by the author, September 2, 2014.

3. https://www.azlyrics.com/lyrics/billyjoel/allentown.html.
4. MD interview, October 7, 2014.
5. The Ven. Richard I. Cluett, interviewed by the author, July 22–23, 2015.
6. Jim Naughton, interviewed by the author, November 18, 2015.
7. Diocese of Bethlehem archives.
8. Bill Lewellis, interviewed by the author, July 23, 2015.
9. Cluett interview.
10. MD, interviewed by the author, September 16, 2014.
11. Cluett interview.
12. The Rev. Anthony R. Pompa, interviewed by the author, July 23, 2015.
13. Lewellis interview.
14. Cluett interview.
15. MD interview, October 7, 2014.
16. Lewellis interview.
17. Cluett interview.
18. J. Robert Wright, ed., *On Being a Bishop: Papers on Episcopacy from the Moscow Consultation, 1992* (New York: The Church Hymnal Corporation, 1993), VI–VII.
19. "Episcopalians Dialogue with Presiding Bishop," Diocese of Bethlehem press release, May 7, 1988, 3.
20. Amy Dyer, interviewed by the author, February 15, 2017.
21. The Rt. Rev. Walton Empey, interviewed by Amy Dyer, July 26, 2017.
22. MD, class lecture at VTS, September 18, 2014.
23. MD interview, September 2, 2014.
24. Robert C. Wilkins, interviewed by the author, July 23, 2015.
25. MD interview, October 7, 2014.
26. Wilkins interview.
27. Kathy Lauer-Williams, "Bishop Comes Full Circle as He Steps Down from Post," *Morning Call* (Allentown, PA), January 25, 1996.
28. The Rev. T. Scott Allen, interviewed by the author, July 23, 2015.
29. MD, class lecture at VTS, September 18, 2014.
30. Bill Lewellis, "Sent from God: A Man Whose Name Was Mark," Diocese of Bethlehem website, www.diobeth.org.
31. Allen interview.
32. MD, interviewed by the author, September 16, 2014.
33. Kristin Casler, "Sexton Now Faces 4,288 Sex Counts," *Morning Call* (Allentown, PA), April 9, 1992.
34. Bill Lewellis, "An Abused Congregation Seeks Healing," *Diocesan Life*, April 16, 1992.
35. MD interview, September 16, 2014.

36. "Ex-Priest Who Assaulted Boys Dies Imprisoned; Adam Tannous of Whitehall Had Sex with Seven," *Morning Call* (Allentown, PA), October 27, 2000.

37. The Rev. John Wagner, interviewed by the author, August 27, 2015.

38. MD interview, September 16, 2014.

39. Lewellis interview.

40. Jennifer Dyer, interviewed by the author, October 16, 2015.

41. Michael Hamlin, in-person and telephone interviews with Amy Dyer, undated.

42. Bill Lewellis, "Marie Elizabeth Dyer Was an Unfinished Woman," *Morning Call* (Allentown, PA), November 25, 1991.

43. Cluett interview.

44. Ibid.

45. Episcopal Church archives, "A Chronology of Events Concerning Women in Holy Orders in the Episcopal Church, USA and the World-wide Anglican Communion," http://arc.episcopalchurch.org/women/two/chronology.htm.

46. Episcopal News Service, "Eleven Women Ordained Episcopal Priests," July 31, 1974.

47. Episcopal Church archives, "Ordination of Women," https://www.episcopalchurch.org/library/glossary/ordination-women.

48. Episcopal Church archives, "A Chronology of Events."

49. MD, class lecture at VTS, September 4, 2014.

50. The Very Rev. Robyn Szoke-Coolidge, interviewed by the author, November 29, 2016.

51. Donald Blount, "Church Embraces AIDS Victims: Service Offers Understanding," *Morning Call* (Allentown, PA), November 25, 1991.

52. Allen interview.

53. MD interview, October 7, 2014.

54. Allen interview.

55. Blount, "Church Embraces AIDS Victims."

56. Allen interview.

57. Former Presiding Bishop Frank T. Griswold, interviewed by the author, February 13, 2016.

58. Peter Steinfels, "Lesbian Ordained Episcopal Priest," *The New York Times*, June 6, 1991.

59. MD statement, Diocese of Bethlehem archives, June 6, 1991.

60. MD statement, Diocese of Bethlehem archives.

61. MD, "Instead of Justice, More Injustice," pastoral letter to the Episcopal Diocese of Bethlehem, November 1984.

62. MD, "Spirituality and the Environment," remarks to the Environmental Task Force of the Diocese of Bethlehem, Spring 1990.
63. The Rt. Rev. Sean Rowe, interviewed by the author, January 6, 2016.
64. MD interview, September 16, 2014.
65. Cluett interview.
66. Allen interview.
67. Rowe interview.
68. Naughton interview.
69. Wilkins interview.
70. Lewellis, "Sent from God."

Chapter 9

1. MD, class lecture at VTS, September 25, 2014.
2. The Most Rev. Dr. Robin Eames, interviewed by the author and Amy Dyer, July 18, 2016.
3. MD interview, September 2, 2014.
4. Tim Reeves, "Dyer to Help Resolve World Conflict Over Women Bishops," *Morning Call* (Allentown, PA), September 22, 1988.
5. Eames interview.
6. Ibid.
7. MD, interview with the author, October 28, 2014.
8. Former Archbishop of Canterbury Rowan Williams, interviewed by the author and Amy Dyer, July 20, 2016.
9. MD, class lecture at VTS, September 18, 2014.
10. MD, class lecture at VTS, September 4, 2014.
11. Williams interview.
12. The Rt. Rev. Gregory Cameron, interviewed by Amy Dyer, July 25, 2016.
13. Williams interview.
14. The Rev. Dr. James Farwell, interviewed by the author, November 13, 2016.
15. The Rt. Rev. David Hamid, interviewed by the author and Amy Dyer, July 21, 2016.
16. The Rev. Canon John Gibaut, interviewed by the author and Amy Dyer, July 21, 2016.
17. Ibid.
18. Cameron interview.
19. Hamid interview.
20. Cameron interview.

21. Williams interview.
22. Gibaut interview.
23. Ibid.
24. Hamid interview.
25. Cameron interview.
26. International Commission for Anglican-Orthodox Theological Dialogue, *The Church of the Triune God: The Cyprus Agreed Statement* (London: The Anglican Communion Office, 2006), 88.
27. Cameron interview.
28. Gibaut interview.
29. Dr. Timothy F. Sedgwick, interviewed by the author, September 30, 2016.
30. Williams interview.

Chapter 10

1. MD, interviewed by the author, September 23, 2014.
2. George Carey, *Know the Truth: A Memoir* (London: HarperCollins, 2004), 331.
3. Anglican Consultative Council, *The Eames Commission: The Official Reports; The Archbishop of Canterbury's Commission on Communion and Women in the Episcopate* (Toronto: Anglican Book Centre, 1994), 11.
4. Ibid.
5. Steve Weston, Episcopal News Service, September 25, 1989.
6. MD, interviewed by the author, September 11, 2014.
7. Jim Naughton, interviewed by the author, November 18, 2015.
8. The Most Rev. Dr. Robin Eames, interviewed by the author and Amy Dyer, July 18, 2016.
9. Naughton interview.
10. Carey, *Know the Truth*, 332.
11. The Rt. Rev. David Hamid, interviewed by the author and Amy Dyer, July 21, 2016.
12. MD, interviewed by the author, September 16, 2014.
13. The Rt. Rev. Sean Rowe, interviewed by the author, January 6, 2016.
14. Former Presiding Bishop Katharine Jefferts Schori, interviewed by the author, April 21, 2016.
15. The Rev. Canon John Gibaut, interviewed by the author and Amy Dyer, July 21, 2016.

Chapter 11

1. MD, interviewed by the author, September 23, 2014.
2. Marc Lacey and Laurie Goodstein, "African Anglican Leaders Outraged Over Gay Bishop in U.S.," *The New York Times*, November 4, 2003.
3. Ibid.
4. Anglican Communion, *The Official Report of the Lambeth Conference 1998* (Harrisburg, PA: Morehouse Publishing, 1998), 381.
5. Lambeth Commission on Communion, "The Windsor Report" (London: The Anglican Communion Office, 2004), 8.
6. Former Archbishop of Canterbury Rowan Williams, interviewed by the author and Amy Dyer, July 20, 2016.
7. The Rt. Rev. Gregory Cameron, interviewed by Amy Dyer, July 25, 2016.
8. The Most Rev. Dr. Robin Eames, interviewed by the author and Amy Dyer, July 18, 2016.
9. Cameron interview.
10. Eames interview.
11. Cameron interview.
12. Lambeth Commission on Communion, "The Windsor Report," 5–6.
13. Ibid.
14. Episcopal News Service, "From Bishop Mark Dyer: Statement on the Windsor Report," October 18, 2004.
15. MD, class lecture at VTS, September 11, 2014.
16. Jim Naughton, interviewed by the author, November 18, 2015.
17. Ibid.
18. Dr. Jenny Te Paa Daniel, interviewed by the author by email, fall 2016 and spring 2017.
19. Te Paa Daniel, July 11, 2009, speech to the House of Deputies at the Episcopal Church's 76th General Convention.
20. The Most Rev. Barry Morgan, interviewed by the author and Amy Dyer, July 21, 2016.
21. Te Paa Daniel interview.
22. Morgan interview.
23. The Rt. Rev. Sean Rowe, interviewed by the author, January 13, 2017.
24. The Rt. Rev. Peter James Lee, interviewed by the author, January 25, 2017.
25. Williams interview.
26. The Very Rev. Dr. Ian S. Markham, interviewed by the author, October 19, 2015.

27. The Very Rev. Dr. Martha J. Horne, interviewed by the author, January 10, 2017.
28. Eames interview.
29. Dr. Mary Tanner, interviewed by Amy Dyer, October 2016.
30. The Rev. Canon John Gibaut, interviewed by the author and Amy Dyer, July 21, 2016.
31. Former Archbishop of Canterbury George Carey, interviewed by Amy Dyer, October 26, 2016.
32. The Rt. Rev. David Hamid, interviewed by the author and Amy Dyer, July 21, 2016.
33. Cameron interview.
34. Williams interview.
35. Morgan interview.

Chapter 12

1. MD, class lecture at VTS, September 4, 2014.
2. MD, "Doing Theology in a Covenant Community: Faith Seeking Understanding," 1994.
3. MD, class lecture at VTS, September 11, 2014.
4. The Rev. Dr. James Farwell, interviewed by the author, November 13, 2016.
5. The Rev. Dr. Helen Appelberg, interviewed by the author, March 6, 2017.
6. Dr. Timothy F. Sedgwick, interviewed by the author, September 30, 2016.
7. Former Presiding Bishop Frank T. Griswold, interviewed by the author, February 13, 2016.
8. Ibid.
9. The Most Rev. Barry Morgan, interviewed by the author and Amy Dyer, July 21, 2016.
10. MD, interviewed by the author, September 30, 2014.
11. Former Archbishop of Canterbury Rowan Williams, interviewed by the author and Amy Dyer, July 20, 2016.
12. Mark Dyer, "Church: A Safe Place for All People," *Episcopal Life*, October 1994: 26.
13. Mark Dyer, "It's Time for an Ecclesiastical Yard Sale," *Episcopal Life*, July 1994: 18.
14. Dyer, "Doing Theology in a Covenant Community."

15. Mark Dyer, "Seek First the Vision of God," convention address, Diocese of Bethlehem archives, December 2, 1995.
16. The Rev. Dr. Katherine Grieb, interviewed by the author, December 30, 2016.
17. The Rev. Javier (Jay) Alanis, interviewed by the author, February 14, 2017.
18. The Rt. Rev. Shannon Johnston, interviewed by the author, December 9, 2016.
19. Confidential source, interviewed by the author, March 8, 2017.
20. The Rev. Andrew T.P. Merrow, interviewed by the author, May 25, 2016.
21. The Rev. Judith Proctor, interviewed by the author, September 27, 2016.
22. The Rev. Oran Warder, interviewed by the author, September 27, 2016.

Chapter 13

1. Kathy Lauer-Williams, "Bishop Comes Full Circle as He Steps Down from Post," *Morning Call* (Allentown, PA), January 25, 1996.
2. The Rev. Dr. Katherine Grieb, interviewed by the author, December 30, 2016.
3. The Very Rev. Dr. Martha J. Horne, interviewed by the author, January 10, 2017.
4. Grieb interview.
5. The Rt. Rev. Peter James Lee, interviewed by the author, January 25, 2017.
6. The Rev. Jacques Hadler Jr., interviewed by the author, October 13, 2016.
7. Dr. Timothy F. Sedgwick, interviewed by the author, September 30, 2016.
8. Horne interview.
9. Sedgwick interview.
10. Mary Lewis Hix, interviewed by the author, November 13, 2016.
11. Former Presiding Bishop Frank T. Griswold, interviewed by the author, February 13, 2016.
12. The Very Rev. William S. Stafford, interviewed by the author, January 10, 2017.
13. The Rev. Mike Angell, interviewed by the author and Amy Dyer, October 4, 2016.
14. Horne interview.
15. The Rt. Rev. Sean Rowe, interviewed by the author, January 6, 2016.
16. Salih Sayilgan, interviewed by the author, April 7, 2016.
17. Zeyneb Sayilgan, interviewed by the author, April 7, 2016.
18. Halim Shukair, interviewed by the author, April 7, 2016.

19. The Rev. Joseph Constant, interviewed by the author, March 13, 2017.
20. Anne McConney, "Episcopal Seminaries Attend to Their Students' Spirits," Episcopal News Service, April 3, 1997.
21. The Rev. Canon Jeunée Godsey, interviewed by the author and Amy Dyer, October 13, 2015.
22. Sedgwick interview.
23. The Rev. Dr. James Farwell, interviewed by the author, November 13, 2016.
24. Grieb interview.
25. The Rt. Rev. Shannon Johnston, interviewed by the author, December 9, 2016.
26. Horne interview.
27. The Rev. Bret B. Hays, interviewed by the author and Amy Dyer, October 4, 2016.
28. Angell interview.
29. Ibid.
30. The Very Rev. Phoebe A. Roaf, interviewed by the author and Amy Dyer, October 4, 2016.
31. The Rev. Wendy Wilkinson, interviewed by the author and Amy Dyer, October 5, 2016.
32. The Rev. Mark Wilkinson, interviewed by the author and Amy Dyer, October 5, 2016.
33. The Rev. Dr. Allison St. Louis, interviewed by the author, October 13, 2016.
34. The Rev. Michael McManus, email to the author, April 28, 2016.
35. Grieb interview.
36. Horne interview.
37. Constant interview.
38. The Rev. Dr. Robert W. Prichard, interviewed by the author, November 16, 2016.
39. The Rev. Dr. Judy Fentress-Williams, interviewed by the author, February 13, 2017.
40. MD, class lecture at VTS, September 4, 2014.
41. Dr. Ellen F. Davis, interviewed by the author, February 3, 2017.
42. Constant interview.
43. The Rev. Dr. Richard J. Jones, interviewed by the author, November 13, 2016.
44. Sedgwick interview.
45. Stafford interview.
46. The Rev. Dr. Katherine Sonderegger, interviewed by the author, November 4, 2016.

47. The Rev. Dr. Lloyd Lewis, interviewed by the author, March 20, 2017.
48. Hadler interview.
49. The Rev. Dr. David T. Gortner, interviewed by the author, March 10, 2017.
50. Fentress-Williams interview.
51. The Rt. Rev. James J. (Bud) Shand, interviewed by the author, November 11, 2015.
52. Lee interview.
53. Shand interview.
54. Johnston interview.
55. Davis interview.

Chapter 14

1. Mary Lewis Hix, interviewed by the author, November 13, 2016.
2. The Ven. Richard I. Cluett, interviewed by the author, July 22–23, 2015.
3. Jennifer Dyer, interviewed by the author, October 16, 2015.
4. The Rt. Rev. Peter James Lee, interviewed by the author, January 25, 2017.
5. The Very Rev. William S. Stafford, interviewed by the author, January 10, 2017.
6. Dr. Ellen F. Davis, interviewed by the author, February 3, 2017.
7. Hix interview.
8. The Rev. Canon Blake Rider, interviewed by the author and Amy Dyer, October 13, 2015.
9. The Rev. Mark Wilkinson, interviewed by the author and Amy Dyer, October 5, 2016.

Chapter 15

1. Amy Dyer, interviewed by the author, February 15, 2017.
2. Ibid.
3. Ibid.
4. The Rev. Dr. Judy Fentress-Williams, interviewed by the author, February 13, 2017.
5. Amy Dyer interview.
6. The Rt. Rev. James J. (Bud) Shand, interviewed by the author, November 11, 2015.

7. Amy Dyer interview.
8. Robyn Gearey, interviewed by the author, October 27, 2016.
9. Amanda Gearey, interviewed by the author, October 3, 2016.
10. The Rev. Dr. Robert W. Prichard, interviewed by the author, November 16, 2016.
11. The Very Rev. William S. Stafford, interviewed by the author, January 10, 2016.

Chapter 16

1. The Rev. Christopher H. Miller, interviewed by the author, February 20, 2017.
2. Amy Dyer, interviewed by the author, February 15, 2017.
3. Robyn Gearey, interviewed by the author, October 27, 2016.
4. Amy Dyer, written statement to the author, June 21, 2017.
5. Amy Dyer interview.
6. MD, class lecture at VTS, September 4, 2014.
7. MD, class lecture at VTS, September 25, 2014.
8. Miller interview.
9. The Rt. Rev. Shannon Johnston, interviewed by the author, December 9, 2016.
10. Amy Dyer interview.
11. Former Archbishop of Canterbury Rowan Williams, interviewed by the author and Amy Dyer, July 20, 2016.

Chapter 17

1. Frederick Buechner, *Listening to Your Life* (New York: HarperCollins, 1992).
2. Former Presiding Bishop Frank T. Griswold, interviewed by the author, February 13, 2016.
3. The Rt. Rev. Sean Rowe, speaking at a tribute to MD at the 144th convention of the Diocese of Bethlehem, October 2, 2015.
4. The Very Rev. Dr. Martha J. Horne, interviewed by the author, January 10, 2017.
5. Sermon by Martha Horne, November 20, 2014.
6. Dr. Ellen F. Davis, interviewed by the author, February 3, 2017.
7. The Very Rev. William S. Stafford, interviewed by the author, January 10, 2016.

8. The Rt. Rev. Shannon Johnston, interviewed by the author, December 9, 2016.

9. The Most Rev. Barry Morgan, interviewed by the author and Amy Dyer, July 21, 2016.

10. The Rev. Dr. Lloyd Lewis, interviewed by the author, March 20, 2017.

11. Griswold interview.

12. Former Archbishop of Canterbury George Carey, interviewed by Amy Dyer, October 26, 2016.

13. Johnston interview.

14. The Most Rev. Desmond Tutu, statement to the author via email, March 17, 2017.

15. The Most Rev. Njongonkulu Ndungane, statement to the author via email, May 31, 2017.

16. The Rt. Rev. Gregory Cameron, interviewed by Amy Dyer, July 25, 2016.

17. The Most Rev. Dr. Robin Eames, interviewed by the author and Amy Dyer, July 18, 2016.

18. The Rev. Dr. Roger Ferlo, interviewed by the author, May 4, 2017.

19. The Rt. Rev. David Hamid, interviewed by the author and Amy Dyer, July 21, 2016.

20. Stafford interview.

21. Former Archbishop of Canterbury Rowan Williams, interviewed by the author and Amy Dyer, July 20, 2016.

22. Jim Naughton, interviewed by the author, November 18, 2015.

23. The Rev. Canon Samuel Van Culin, interviewed by the author and Amy Dyer, June 24, 2016.

24. The Rt. Rev. Sean Rowe, interviewed by the author, January 6, 2016.

25. The Very Rev. Dr. Ian S. Markham, statement to the author via email, April 23, 2017.

26. Davis interview.

27. Stafford interview.

BIBLIOGRAPHY

Anglican Communion. *The Official Report of the Lambeth Conference 1998*. Harrisburg, PA: Morehouse Publishing, 1998.

Anglican Consultative Council. *The Truth Shall Make You Free: The Lambeth Conference 1988, the Reports, Resolutions and Pastoral Letters from the Bishops*. London: Church House Publishing, 1988.

Anglican Consultative Council. *The Eames Commission: The Official Reports; The Archbishop of Canterbury's Commission on Communion and Women in the Episcopate*. Toronto: Anglican Book Centre, 1994.

Archives of the Episcopal Church. Minutes of the House of Bishops, 1994 General Convention of the Episcopal Church.

Bass, Diana Butler. *Strength for the Journey: A Pilgrimage of Faith in Community*. New York: Church Publishing, 2017.

Buchanan, Colin. *Historical Dictionary of Anglicanism*. Lanham, MD: Scarecrow Press, 2006.

Carey, Eileen, with Andrew Carey. *The Bishop and I: Taking the Lid Off the Church's Best-Kept Secret*. London: Hodder & Stoughton, 1998.

Carey, George. *Know the Truth: A Memoir.* London: HarperCollins, 2004.

Chadwick, Owen. *Michael Ramsey: A Life.* Oxford: Clarendon Press, 1990.

De Waal, Esther. *Seeking God: The Way of St. Benedict.* Collegeville, MN: Liturgical Press, 1984.

Dyer, Mark. "Doing Theology in a Covenant Community: Faith Seeking Understanding." 1994.

Gibaut, John. "A Tale of Two Ecclesiologies: The Church of the Triune God and The Church: Towards a Common Vision." Toronto: Trinity College, 2013.

Hastings, Max. *The Korean War.* New York/Cambridge: Simon & Schuster, 1987.

Inter-Anglican Theological and Doctrinal Commission. "The Virginia Report." Harrisburg, PA: Morehouse Publishing, 1998.

International Commission for Anglican-Orthodox Theological Dialogue. *The Church of the Triune God: The Cyprus Agreed Statement.* London: The Anglican Communion Office, 2006.

Kujawa-Holbrook, Sheryl A. *The Heart of a Pastor: A Life of Edmond Lee Browning.* Cincinnati: Forward Movement, 2010.

Lambeth Commission on Communion. "The Windsor Report." London: The Anglican Communion Office, 2004.

"Manchester Memories: The Early Years." *New Hampshire Union Leader,* 2012.

Marty, Martin. *The Christian World: A Global History.* New York: The Modern Library, 2007.

Merton, Thomas. *The Seven Storey Mountain: An Autobiography of Faith.* New York: Harcourt, 1948.

Miller, David. "Memoirs of a Draft-Card Burner." *Reclaiming Quarterly,* Spring 2001. Reclaimingquarterly.org.

Prichard, Robert. *A History of the Episcopal Church,* 3rd ed. Nashville, TN: Abingdon, 2014.

Riegle, Rosalie G. *Crossing the Line: Nonviolent Resisters Speak Out for Peace.* Eugene, OR: Cascade Books, 2013.

Rosenthal, James, ed. *The Essential Guide to the Anglican Communion.* Harrisburg, PA: Morehouse Publishing, 1998.

Rothman, Lily. "It Was 50 Years Ago that David Miller Lit the Flame." *Time.com*, October 15, 2015.

Sears, David. *Such Men as These: The Story of the Navy Pilots Who Flew the Deadly Skies over Korea.* Cambridge, MA: Da Capo Press, 2010.

Shortt, Rupert. *Rowan's Rule: The Biography of the Archbishop of Canterbury.* Grand Rapids, MI: William B. Eerdmans Publishing Company, 2008.

Sparks, Allister, and Mpho Tutu. *Tutu: Authorized.* Auckland: HarperOne, 2011.

Thompson, Warren. *F9F Panther Units of the Korean War.* Oxford: Osprey Publishing, 2014.

"USS *Bennington*: Ship's History: December 15, 1941–December 31, 1955." Department of the Navy.

Webber, Elizabeth B. *On This Rock: Christ Church of Hamilton and Wenham.* Privately published, undated.

Wright, J. Robert, ed. *On Being a Bishop: Papers on Episcopacy from the Moscow Consultation, 1992.* New York: The Church Hymnal Corporation, 1993.

INDEX

Printed in the USA
CPSIA information can be obtained
at www.ICGtesting.com
LVHW051808080224
771345LV00005B/1029

9 781640 650978